Aftermath-Survival

Concrete Jungle Ultimate Lessons

Frank Marchante

Grass Publishing, Miami, Florida

Aftermath-Survival Concrete Jungle Ultimate Lessons

All rights reserved. Printed in the United States of America. *Except as permitted under the United States Copyright Act* of 1976. No part of this publication may be reproduced or distributed in any form or by any means, or stored in a database or retrieval system, without the prior written permission of the publisher.

Published by Gras Publishing Company
www.graspublishing.com
Miami, Florida, 33155

Copyright © 2024 Frank Marchante

Cover Photographs
Men wearing Hoodie-Darksouls1 Pixabay.com
Men Running-MariaD42530 Pixabay.com
Men with rifle-Frank Marchante
Back Cover Photographs
Roasting Pixeldust Pixabay.com
Men in ruin building -Andrew Amistad Unplash.com
City skyline in fire-Stockgiu Freepick.com

Library of Congress Control Number: 2023923309
Marchante, Frank
P. 310
ISBN-978-0-9779040-7-5
613.8'5-dc22

This book is printed in Acid free paper.
United States -
Printed in the United States of America

1-Urban Survival 2-Martial Law 3-Economic Collapse 4- Nuclear survival 5- Guide Education survivals

Dedication

To my mother, I credit everything I have achieved in life to her love, moral, intellectual and education she gave me. She was always there to advice, supported and encouraged me all my life and still does, even after many years have passed since she passed away, she continues to encourage and inspire me. She was my best friend; I share all my secrets and could talk freely with her on any matter.

I would also want to dedicate this book to my late father, whose love and advice will live on in me forever. He was my teacher, confident, a role model, but most of all, he was my best friend. Thanks to my dad and my mother, for making me who I am.

In addition, I want to honor my sister by dedicating this book to my sister Babie, who is the most dependable and wisest helper someone could have. She deserves a special mention in this book. By having sisters like her, you keep alive your past. They're the only ones listening, if you talk about your memories.

I also want to dedicate this book to my son Franky, who encourage and helped me comprehend the danger of and the importance of being prepared for a SHTF situation.

"A father is someone you look up to no matter how tall you grow"
Unknown

Warning-Disclaimer

Disclaimer

The materials presented in this book are for "informational and entertainment purposes only", and in no way should be used as a substitute for actual instruction. To participate in any physical activity, you should consult your physician and ask for a complete exam, and agree to be of legal age and use the information responsibly.

The author and publisher are providing you with information for your educational knowledge only. Be aware that if you follow any of the advice included in this book, you are doing so entirely at your own risk, consisting of all past, present, or any future physical, medical, or psychological pain or injury whatsoever that you may incur or receive.

The author and publisher will not suggested accuracy, validity and reliability for the information on this book. Under no circumstance the author or publisher will have any liability for loss or damage of any kind as a result of any information provided in this book.

The ownership of some weapons is restricted by states and federals laws. Before acquiring and using weapons the reader should learn about the laws complying about weapons.

This book does not contain medical-health advice, the information is only provided as general information for educational purpose only, and it is not substitute for your doctor professional advice.

Information obtained by websites/ magazine were not investigated, monitored or checked for accuracy and reliability. The author and publisher do not assume responsibility or reliability offered by them.

We are simply providing information that may or not be useful to others. The author and publisher should bear no liability or responsibility to any person or entity for any loss or damage caused, or alleged to be caused, directly or indirectly by the information in this book.

This book contains only the author's personal opinions.

Acknowledgement

I want to give special recognition to my son Franky, who introduced me to prepping, Teotwawki, the end of the world as we know it, the apocalypse, or SHTF, and how to be ready in case of an Catastrophe.

Franky seeing you grow fills me with immense pride. I admire the creatives' ideas you have. You may be a man to everyone else, but you still my boy to me. The day you were born, was one of the happiest days in my life.

You are the only one man I love, my one and only son. Thanks for always been there, you are a great friend. I'm a proud father.

Also, I will like to thank my daughter Michelle for helping me design this book cover.

I like to mention my wife for being my biggest supporter and best friend who has stood by me through all these years. Also thanks to my three children-Monica-Franky-Michelle-who have brought so much joy into my live.

A special thanks to all the magazines writers, publications, websites, Park Rangers, and survival experts whose concepts I incorporated into this book and expanded upon. I'm grateful to all those people, and the sources who gave me interview. It will be challenging to list every one of them.

Thanks to all!

Danger behind every corner after a SHTF catastrophe

Table of content

Introduction

Lesson 1-page 20

Survivalist & prepper
Global Pandemic
What is the Apocalypse?
Social and economic Collapse
Surviving mob/Gangs
Mayor Catastrophe
Martial law
Shelter
Civil unrest
No law enforcement
The authorities will try to take your guns.

Lesson 2-page 33

Bug in or out danger
Benefits of bugging in
Situations to bug out
Bug out shelter list
Concrete jungle
Risk in the city
Urban survival
The power Grid
Escapes
Everglades
Waste in the neighborhood

Lesson 3-page 48

Home
Fortify your perimeter
Fortifying the home
SHTF three requirements
Safe room
Martial Law
Dogs
Backyard Livestock
Blocking your driveway and your street
Sex slave prisoners
Be invisible to thugs
Neighborhood security
Different Booby traps
Nighttime
Home security 24/7
Going alone

Lesson 4-page 68

Lose a tracking dog
Gray man
Camouflage at night
Local weather
Bury yourself
Gray woman
Learn to be alone
Woman and guns
Pregnancy
Sex-Prostitution

Lesson 5-page 78

Moving as a squat
Skills for Scouts
Operating Procedures
Evasion
Scouts Assets
Walkie-talkie

No cameo
Signaling
Navigation
River crossing
Skills to survive

Lesson 6-page 91

Ambushes
Sleeping location
Rooftops
Escape routes
Self-defense
Cathole

Snow walking
Treat gunshot wounds
Survival actions
Recovery tactics for vehicles
Destructive devices
Safety

Lesson 7-page 104

Bartering
Best bartering items
Scavenger
Basic scavenging
Places to scavenging
Communication
Morse code

Transportation
Bicycle-Motor Bike- Moped
Motorcycle-Truck-Car
Boat-Canoe-Kayak
Non-engine-powered vehicles
Horses, etc.
Walking

Lesson 8- page 126

Drone
Cross-country trip after SHTF
Items to take for this trip
In your person
In your backpack
Bikes attach

Danger every turn you take
Blocked Highway
Main roads
Roundtrip
Not wise to make such a trip

Lesson 9-page 131

Specific survival weapons
AR-15
.22 rifles
AK- 47
Automatic Pistols-9mm Luger
Revolvers-357 magnum-.38
Pump Shotgun-12- 20 gauge
.410 shells
Winchester- .30-30
Bulletproof vests
BB Guns-pellet guns
Slingshots-The Bow

Crossbow
Machetes, knifes
Tactical knife
Tomahawk-Hatchet- Ax
Spear
Items for defense
Fire extinguishers / weapon
Lubrication
Gun handling
Safely store a gun

Lesson 10-147

Water
Solar water disinfection
Rainwater collection
Precaution
Regret not having when SHTF
Survival Checklist
Canned food expiration date
Prisoners in SHTF

Health
First aid
Natural remedies
Antibiotic
Types of bleeding
Tourniquet
Monitor the wound for infection

Lesson 11- page 154

Refrigeration
Root cellar-Zeer pot
Cooking-Methods of cooking
Rock cooking
Build a mud oven
Build Hobo Stove
Dehydrating food-Safety
Canned food
Keep food Long time
List to storage food
Sand to keep food cool

Vegetable garden
Tin can remove
Food poisoning symptoms
Long-term food companies
Learn Hand-fishing
Spearfishing-Ice Fishing
Ice thickness chart
Cleaning the fish
Looter-criminal and pillager will look for

Lesson 12-page 168

Heat
Water filter
Rain collection system
How to wash clothes
Soap-making
Knife Sharpening

Home Garbage
Items you should
Hide when SHTF
Toilets
Make a Latrine
Make a Outhouse

Lesson 13-page 174

Skills for end of the World
First Aid
Gunsmithing
Teacher-Doctor-Midwife
Skills You Must Know
Poor sanitation
Age average-Skin Cancer
Infection
Resuscitation and first aid

Remedies relieve tooth pain
Tooth removal-Door knob
Pliers system
Eye Glasses
Neighborhood waste
Showers-Shaving
Plants for toilet paper-Portable
Toilets
Bucket toilet system-Latrines

Lesson 14-page 186

Pandemic
Rules of first aid
Superglue-wounds
Broken bone
Symptoms broken bone
Burns

Minor cuts
Minor Punctures
Survive the apocalypse with
kids
Wild medicinal plants
Avoiding poisonous plants

Lesson 15-page 195

Apartment-Condominium
Microtrees-stockpile
Non-perishable-Dehydrated food
The elevator
Balcony Advantage
Food not require storage
Stove-CO- laundry
Firearms
Poop, urine, trash, fire danger

Perimeter
Collapsible Water containers
Toolbox, emergency-lights
Fire options option
Devices to escape
Poisoning-symptoms
Pets
Two-bucket toilet

Lesson 16-page 208

Goal list
Home-grow
Communications
Transportation
Health -first aid
Sanitation, Clothing and cleanliness
Entertaining
Important papers

Stockpile items
Stockpile photos 1-2-3
Homemade laundry detergent
How to make detergent
How to Make a Solar Oven
Open a can without a can opener
A 2- little bottle uses

Lesson 17-page 219

9 best household animals for urban homesteading
Birds-Chicken
Baby chicks
Male or female chick
Tell if a chick is a rooster
Hen eggs without a rooster
Roost space
Size-build a small coop
Ducks
Edible games in the city

Quail-Quail cage
Rabbits-Hutch
Killing rabbits humanely
The most humane methods
Turkeys-Pheasants
 Enclosure-cage
 Pigs-Goats-Sheep
 Backyard animal's photos
 Eating Lizards

Lesson 18-page 238

The Truth-hunting-fishing
Mountain survival
Sleeping in the mountain
Survive a lighting storm
Everglades-Florida
Dangerous animals in Florida
Survival spear
How to make a spear
The Desert
What is a desert?

Desert Survival
Finding water in the desert
Can you drink your own pee?
Predators in the desert
Bee Stings
Remedies for Bee stings
Insects and Arachnids
Wasps and hornets
Poisonous Snakes of the Americas

Lesson 19-page 262

Animals' attacks
Red Wolves and Coyotes
Avoid triggering an attack
Cougars and bobcats
Bears-survive a bear attack

Rodents and small animals
Foxes and raccoons
Bats
Cat bite
Dogs

Lesson 20-page 267

Death Body
Backyard to bury the dead
How to handle a dead body
Protective gear
Transporting the body

Risk of handling dead bodies
Burning the dead
Procedure without equipment
Serious disease outbreak

BOOK # 2 **Future Education survival**

This guide provides the teacher or person in charge with schooling children's history lesson plans, with tips and step by step to a Homeschool planner guide -From Kindergarten thru12th grade

Section 1 page 270

Education for future survival
Skills for staying alive
History
Influential Documents in
American History
The Founding Fathers
Presidents of the United States

Abraham Lincoln
John F. Kennedy
Ronald Wilson Reagan
Barack Hussein Obama
Donald John Trump
Joe Biden

Section 2 page 278

Assassination in the U.S.A
Wars-USA Wars
American Generals
History in time
Disaster Bay of Pig
Communist head of state

American Astronauts
First American man in space
First American orbit the earth
Apollo 11-landing in the moon
Apollo 13 aborted touchdown
Aldrin moon foot print

Section 3 page 288

Basic Computer World
Microsoft
Apple Computer
MicroPro International
IBM's first personal computer
Microsoft releases Windows
Google search

Wi-Fi
The MacBook Pro
The iPad
Apple Watch
World Wide Web

Section 4 page 290

Music revolution
Major Pop star list
Elvis Presley-the King
The Beatles

Section 5 page 294

Homeschool planner guide example

Differentiation in elementary, middle, and high school.
These skills are needed by all children in order to learn how to read.
Kindergarten
1th grade
2th grade
3rd grade
4th grade
5th grade
6th grade
7th grade

8th grade
9th grade
10th grades
11th grades
12th grade

Tutors after the catastrophe

Final Thoughts page	298
SHTF Terminologies	299
Author page	302
Photo credit page	304-305
Informational Websites	305
Grass publishing books	306-307-308-309
Notes page	310

Preface

The purpose of this book is to provide you, the reader, with the knowledge you will need to survive and defend yourself and your family. This is a hands-on course at every level, while trying not to repeat how to survive like many other books. It's an easy-to-read book that places information at your fingertip.

Here's the harsh reality: in a SHTF scenario, the path ahead will be very dangerous. That seems grim, and it certainly will be. To ensure that you and your family survive, you must focus and take every necessary action.

First, let me tell you about myself. I'm a father, grandfather, a retired teacher, hunter, pilot, an avid reader, and a writer. I'm writing this book as an average man on the street, smart and capable but not an expert military, police, or soldier. This is a book on how to survive and get ready if there is a social collapse.

This book focuses on surviving in the suburbs of the city. However, I have included the Everglades, the mountains, and the desert for those of you thinking about a bug-out destination.

As a young boy, I remember exploring the deep forestland with the woods a short distance from my home-farm. Early on, I learned how to use and shoot a variety of various firearms. I've been an avid hunter in the Florida Everglades for more than 40 years.

I have spent thousands of hours hunting; does that make me an expert in the Everglades? No, it doesn't; I have also hunted in numerous different areas of the Florida Everglades, occasionally for long hours or days, walking through trails, mangroves, and the swamp with a machete.

In La Paz, Bolivia, the highest city in the world nearly 12,000 above sea level, I was caught up in a dangerous political protest riot, and in a student march in Mexico City, which eventually transformed into a flash political riot during my visit to Mexico City University.

I have not experienced or survived an economic meltdown; however I have experienced difficult circumstances all over the world. I have been in situations where major cities shut down. Like when I returned to La Paz, Bolivia from a jungle trip in an open pickup truck, surrounded side by side with indigenous insurgent's people for about 20 hours during a mayor's violent political demonstration by Bolivians.

Another time I was stuck alone three nights on a deserted mountain top in the Andes of Bolivia, freezing with no running water, heat or electricity, with limited food and drinking water. This area was extremely remote and hard to describe.

Frank in Bolivia

I traveled for days into the heart of the Amazon rainforest, into the dense undergrowth one of the wildest dangerous environments on the planet, extremely deep in the jungle, through the Bolivian Amazon in Bolivia and Peru. I also climbed the Illimani in Bolivia, one of the higher peaks in the Andes, and the Popocatépetl in Mexico City.

Some of my expeditions were extremely difficult and I would not want to repeat them

On a very remote and high peak in the Georgia Mountains, my son purchased a cabin as a bug-out location in case of an emergency.

We hike day and night through the woods in the mountain; we never encountered another person there.

Georgia cabin with son Franky

Being a resident of Miami, Florida which is in the path of several hurricanes, in August 1992, I witnessed firsthand the devastation and felt the destruction of Hurricane Andrew, a category 5 storm. I know first-hand what it's to be afraid, in distress, desolation, and to how overcome it. I also lost my Panther two-seater aircraft on that day.

This event rendered a significant portion of the city's infrastructure utterly inoperable. I also lived through very bad times without electricity for four weeks; we had to improvise and find ways to find gas, food, and supplies.

There is no doubt that the world has changed in the last few years, and the information in this book will serve as a guide for your and your family's survival after the SHTF, no matter your level of training or experience. Adjustment is a crucial part of surviving, being able to adapt and navigate through changing and challenging situations.

It seems like most advice in survival books is for people to bug out or for just a few of them to stay in your house, but there is almost no information for people who live in an apartment. I have studied and implemented survival techniques in my life.

The reason is that living in an apartment is going to be very hard during a collapse situation. Very few articles and books explain how to defend and protect your family in an apartment or condo. This is a very important topic for many people who live there. This is why I wrote and took into consideration advice and a chapter on apartment prepping and surviving.

The end of the world has been announced many times before, but I hope the information contained in this volume based on my experience, also includes advice from interviews with expert's outdoor enthusiasts, survival experts in several fields, Florida Park Rangers, Police officers, and data and information learned from hundreds of articles and books read on the subject.

I was in Cuba in 1959 during the Castro revolution, and I saw firsthand when hell overnight took place. As a very young boy, I witnessed the mobs move into the city, looting and breaking into homes and buildings.

I saw two young dead bodies up close at the age of eight when the Cuban Revolution was taking place. My eyes have seen things that I believe have given me the experience and idea for this book. As a young boy I saw first-hand the crisis and reprisals of the invasion of Bay of Pigs in Cuba.

The greatest risk I faced when I was growing up was that of a nuclear war.

The Cuban Missile Crisis in 1962 was undoubtedly the closest we came to a nuclear war. I remember we used to do a drill in a Miami, Florida, school of a nuclear attack, and we had to hide under the students' desks (like that was going to help).

The recommendations in this book may now be prohibited in any national park like the Everglades, but in a catastrophe, the only laws that will matter will be the laws of survival: national wildlife refuges, state lands, and private lands will all be of logical use.

Given the sequence of recent shootings, civil unrest, medical emergencies and natural disasters, a lot of experts think the question is not if it will happen, but rather when.

I don't believe that the end of the world will happen; I believe it will be the end of the world as we know it now. Many people believe that most of us will act with kindness instead of brutality. Others believe that in large cities, predators and gangs will take advantage and incite mobs to do unlawful acts.

A few years ago, people mocked anyone who was getting ready or stockpiling foods and general supplies for their family. Today, those people understood what happens with the COVID-19 virus and how panicked the 2020 toilet paper crisis was.

Organizations like the Red Cross recommends American to keep extra food and emergency supplies, for example, The federal Emergency Management Agency (FEMA) recommends to keep two weeks supply of food, water, batteries, medical supplies, and battery powered radio on hands.

It only takes some fear for the crowds to run into stores and get hold of everything they can grab. These are dangerous times; get ready to take action to protect yourself and your loved ones when the time arises, making sure you read this book, pay attention, and apply the information so you can make it through a disaster. The techniques I disclose here are extremely simple, effective, and not confusing.

They are specifically designed for regular everyday people, like you and me. I hope the information discussed here will serve you well. This book was a bear to write; it was very difficult to research and collect information from many separate sources.

The arrangement of this book is easy to follow and will provide guidance that can be used by people of all backgrounds and skill levels.

This book is divided into two parts. In section book #2, a lesson plan guide is included for teaching kids in a catastrophic, from kindergarten through 12th grade, including some basic math, how to read, USA history, and world history. One of the most necessary pieces of information ignored in most survival books is the education of our children and grandchildren after SHTF.

I'm not claiming to be an expert, I'm not. But, I will teach you survival lessons I've learned from my adventure experiences through La Paz Bolivia, Peru, Ecuador, Mexico City, Dominican Republic, New York, Canada, California, New Orleans, Philadelphia, Miami, FL and others cities.

Surviving city specifics can be found in my book Street Wise Extreme-Surviving the Unexpected, Published in 2019. The self-defense tactics, and strategies taught in this book have been successfully employed by women, man, old, weak people, youngsters, and by me.

This book, Aftermath-Survival lessons-The Concrete Jungle Ultimate Survival is ideal for anyone who wants to learn to survive in the streets of today. Surviving in the city after the SHTF is going to be difficult and rough to access to food, water, and medical supplies. Even if the world we know may change, we nevertheless have the obligation to rise the next generation of boys and girls who will take over for us when we get old or pass.

In a catastrophic, frightful situation, you will discover exactly what you're capable of when your family is threatened.

"The future depends on what you do today."
Mahatma Gandhi

Lesson 1

Collapse

There are two circumstances that you will need to plan for. The first is survival during the global collapse.

The second is survival after the collapse. You will also have to create a new way of living after the collapse.

To survive, people will have to change their beliefs, habits, and probably moral views. Houses will be broken as desperate people search for food.

Pharmacies will be looted, and manufacturers will stop producing new supplies for months or years. Some people will get by with herbal medicine, but those requiring level doses of prescription drugs required for life will have a tremendous problem.

You must be prepared to defend your life with weapons. Some people will come together to form gangs so they can take anything they want by force.

What is the difference between a survivalist and a prepper?

The goal of both is to make it through the socio-economic collapse of society. A survivalist work on his survival skills to be ready for an event. The prepper stocks up on resources to survive an event. Prepping occurs before a panic not during a catastrophe.

Survivalists are skilled people; they train themselves in the art of survival. Preppers are all about preparing for disaster. They will stockpile a large amount of resources.

Experts think there are about 15 million Americans actively prepping right now, or about 10% of all households in the United States.

Survivalists have excellent survival skills, while preppers have amazing resources for survival.

TEOTWAWKI–SHTF

They are different. SHTF situations get very frightening for a time, but they eventually return to some normality as time passes by. Teotwawki is a devastating event resulting in a sustained survival condition with a complete breakdown of all existing institutions. Teotwawki for one person may seem like nothing to another.

SHTF, which means Shit Hit the Fan in Teotwawki, means the end of the world as we know it, an expression that a horrible disaster or something big has happened. It may never happen in your lifetime, but if it does, you should want to be prepared so you and your family can survive.

In a SHTF, we will all—men, women, and youngsters—be required to do whatever is necessary to survive. To make it simple for the reader, we'll interchange SHTF and Teotwawki throughout this book.

What is the Apocalypse?

Is the idea of the end of the world as we know it true? The Mayans predicted it was going to happen in 2012, but many experts in the subject claim that probably what it means is that the world is going to change completely as we know it now.

At some point in a Teotwawki disaster, you may be forced to make a decision about who lives and who dies. Only the tough will survive; strong people will die protecting their families and homes.

There are countless ways the apocalypse could happen, even if it never happens. No matter how or when the apocalypse happens, you should be prepared.

Do you really think the US government has no idea about all your card purchases? And have no idea what you have been purchasing for the last couple of years? Think again.

Think about it; it could happen at any time—when you are reading this book, when you wake up in the morning, or when you are taking a shower.

Gangs and muggers

In the event of a total collapse of society, gangs will rise up and kill most men and take their women as slaves. Well-armed gangs will try to quickly take control of major cities. In the past, almost every time people were looting, steeling, and trying to take advantage of a bad situation, once things go really bad, traveling in a city will become a nightmare.

Gangs and bandits will unite to thrive by taking resources from others. They will travel from city to city, raping and robing for their needs.

Gangs or groups will enter a home by force and take anything they want. I'm afraid this will also include attacks on female members in your home, who run the risk of being sex molested or raped and also being taken away. It may sound extreme, but it has happened in the past in other places.

In a crisis, most people have no idea how to survive, and they will become desperate and unpredictable. Most people will become a threat when they are faced with surviving with no knowledge or supplies.

No food left in the stores? What about when there is no gas in the gas station or when they run out of gas?

The water will stop flowing from the tap or may come out contaminated. Water will have to be filtered, and that takes a lot of time.

The average person will be screwed—no power, no water, no food, and no way to communicate. People will become very dangerous. What would you do to feed your family? Things will quickly turn into a disaster.

When the power goes out, no matter the cause—natural disaster or terrorist attack—only then do we realize how dependent we are on electricity.

No law enforcement

Probably they will become nonexistent—officers will need to take care of their own families, facing mass riots, violence, no gas, and empty grocery stores.

Fake law enforcement

People will be impersonating law enforcement and military personnel; criminals will be preying on the innocent by pretending to be police or military personnel. You need to be on the lookout.

The authorities will try to take your guns.

Before and after Hurricane Katrina, the U.S. Marshall and the National Guard troops forcibly confiscated legal firearms from law-abiding citizens.

Most likely, they will come for your guns in a disaster.

Martial law will probably prevail; the presence of the military in your area after a collapse may not even be friendly. They too may be taking what they want by force, including healthy people, to make them work for their communities.

Also, the women are in special danger.

Knowledge

Stays informed and seek out current and relevant information, referring to riots, protests, and crime going on in your immediate area. The more you know about surviving—home security, guns, foods, medicines, weather, and water—the better chance you have to survive.

The brain is the best survival tool we all have.

There are many types of Doomsday argument scenarios that can occur.

Financial depression—fear of social and economic collapse

A financial collapse is the complete failure of the monetary system. Your employer may not be able to pay you. Urban areas may see civil unrest. Avoid crows.

Nuclear War

The United States and Russia even now have about 19,000 active nuclear warheads. Nuclear bombs remain deadly. There is likewise the opportunity for an unintentional nuclear exchange. A nuclear detonation would cause a fatality rate of at least 80 to 90% in the blast zone.

If you live in a major city and there is a catastrophic event like a nuclear weapon detonating within a hundred miles, the entire region will be racing to escape through freeways and highways.

There are six stages to a nuclear blast. There is a flash of lights, a wave of heat, a release of nuclear radiation, a fireball, a blast of air, and finally the radioactive fallout. The flash from a nuclear detonation will last 22 seconds. It takes 10 minutes for the mushroom to attain its full height.

The next danger is the wave from a nuclear attack. Also, the nuclear fallout dust released can cause radiation for up to five weeks or months; clouds will block the sun and kill people months or years afterward.

High-altitude winds can make it sprinkle over hundreds of square miles, and it is most intense near the blast site.

Sheltering in an area for at least 12 to 24 hours is really how long the worst of this radiation lasts, and this can help you continue to survive the chance of fallout.

The best way to be protected before, during, and after a nuclear detonation is to be inside or get inside as quickly as possible.

A solid building will provide the best protection from shock waves, heat, and radiation.

Also, you should be away from windows and doors, and if it has a basement, the better. Use duct tape and plastic sheeting to seal any windows, or vents just in case radiation cloud is passing over.

The lower you go in the building, the more helpful it is, and the farther away you are from windows that can blow apart, doors that can fly open, and outside walls that can cave in, the better your chances.

If you are in an office building, go to an inside stairwell. They are in the core of the building and have concrete walls.

If it caught you outside and you couldn't get to a building, the next best thing to do is to hide in a metro underground.

If you are outside, you will have about 15 minutes to find a place inside to hide before the fallout begins.

Once inside, remove your clothes and shoes right away, take a shower, washing your entire body and hair, blow your nose to remove any inhaled fallout, and flush your eyes, nose, eyebrows, and eyelashes with water or with a wet cloth. And disposes of your contaminated cloth in a sack far away.

Wash any pets that have been outside with cleaning soap and water, and brush your pet's coat to do away with any fallout particles.

Put on uncontaminated clothes.

Vehicles and mobile homes offer almost no protection from nuclear detonation.

It is safe to drink or eat packaged food or items that were inside the building. Do not consume food or liquids that were outdoors; they may be contaminated.

Depending on the level of radioactive particles, a quality filter can last from 30 minutes to a few days before it needs to be replaced.

A good mask will create a seal around your face to ensure the quality of the air you are breathing.

Ideally, a gas mask or respirator rated to NBC standards. NBC stands for Nuclear, Biological, and Chemicals used to refer to protective equipment.

Mask without a filter

Iodine is a powerful remedy for radiation exposure. Iodine can help block radioactive iodine from being absorbed by the thyroid gland, protecting this gland, which is the part of the body that is most sensitive to radioactivity.

Depending on your age, weight, and exposure level, you will want to take distinctive dosages.

See chart:

Age group	Dosage
Adults over18 years old	1 tablet 130mg
Children over 12 years old to 18 years old:	1 tablet 130mg
Children over 3 years old to 18 years	1 tablet 65mg
Weigh less than 150 pounds	
Children over 1 month to 3 years	32.5 mg
Birth to 1 month	16.25 mg

Stay put inside for as long as you can—24 hours or more—and use radios, TV, or telephones if the electricity is still on so you can receive information.

If not, you are going to be on your own, which is why it is a good idea to learn as much as possible before anything like this happens.

Civil War, Civil Unrest, and Riots

People could turn against each other for political, religious, or other reasons.

Gangs and groups

Gangs could attack locals and maybe even attempt to appropriate power and control fuel supplies, supermarkets, warehouses, etc.

Insanity

The World Health Organization calculates that approximately 500 million people across the world have a medical condition related to a psychological disorder.

Global Pandemic

Twice in modern history, plagues have swept the world. The Black Plague killed many people during the 14th century; influenza took at least 20 million lives between 1918 and 1919; the Spanish flu killed more than 50 million people; and the AIDS epidemic has produced a similar death toll and is still going strong. COVID-19 coronavirus. The 2020 lockdown gave us an interesting highlight: a localized collapse.

At the time of this writing, COVID-19 has killed more than 6.80 million people worldwide, including more than 600,000 in the U.S. At the same time, more than 2 billion people worldwide The coronavirus pandemic will change the world forever.

EMP-OR Massive Grid-Down Event

The electric power system may fail due to various reasons, such as a potent solar storm or a nuclear bomb's detonation at high altitude. It is also susceptible to a terrorist cyberattack, which can lead to disastrous consequences.

The outcome of such a failure can be catastrophic, disrupting our modern way of life. Without electricity, we cannot keep our food fresh, pump gas, or regulate our homes' temperature.

We would also lose internet connectivity and possibly phone services. The collapse of the power grid could potentially cripple our entire nation and take several years to recover. This would result in panic, desperation, and an exorbitant rise in the prices of essential commodities like gas, bread, and milk, assuming they are available.

Biotech Disaster

A biological hazard that poses a threat to the health of living organism, primarily humans.

Medical care

Lack of access to basic care for many years, with no medicine or medical drugs. You and your family will need to provide your own medical care, and everyone will need to learn some medical skills to help each other.

Chemical release

It involves the discharge of chemicals into the air ground. Sickening or killing a lot of people.

Asteroid Impact

An asteroid would cause major extinctions. Scientists estimate that's what killed the dinosaurs: particles that blocked the sun for months, causing millions of deaths. On August 11, 2021, at 1.44 p.m. in Cape Canaveral, FL, scientists reported they have a better chance today to deal with an asteroid impact. We don't know the truth about that.

The asteroid known as 2023 SDW was discovered on February 26, 2023. Experts currently estimate that the asteroid has a one-in-400 chance of impacting the Earth. It's predicted that it could impact the Earth on Valentine's Day in 2046. also has the potential to impact from 2047 to 2051, according to the experts risk list.

Earthquake

A large earthquake may destroy your home; power lines may be broken; and gas lines may make you evacuate your home.

Hurricane-Tornado

Common injuries are to limbs, cuts and wounds due to debris falling.

Giant solar flares

Properly known as coronal mass ejections. One threat could not come from a little sun but from too much.

Global Warming

Climate change has been the subject of heated debate and political disputes for years.

Global warming could flood cities and ruin harvests.

Super volcanos

It is another threat. Every 100,000 years or so, there is an eruption with violent exhalations. Volcanic eruptions cause many fatalities.

The aches could asphyxiate people caught underneath.

Mayor earthquakes

An earthquake is a shift within the earth crust. Causing massive damage to infrastructure and the loss of thousands of lives.

Terrorist attacks

Domestic terrorism comes in many different forms. From handmade pipe bombs to mass shootings or vehicles carrying explosives targeting shopping centers, government buildings, and churches.

Over Population

Astrophysicist Stephen Hawking has warned us that overpopulation could lead to the demise of Earth as we know it.

Fear for government control

Government breakdown: losing basic civil liberties and the right to bear arms.

Alien Invasion

Some individuals believe it is conceivable and that it might occur at any time.

A team of scientists at the Mountain View (SETI) Institute in California sifts through radio static in search of a possible signal from an extraterrestrial civilization.

Nothing has happened so far, but inviting more powerful civilizations to visit us could be a mistake because they could turn us into slaves or subjugate us.

The majority of people think they will either never live to see something like this or that nothing like it will ever occur.

Basic information about pandemics:

Smallpox outbreaks linked to European settlers were among the first pandemics in the United States.

Smallpox

In the 1600s, illness wiped out all of the Native American tribes. According to rough estimates, certain tribes had a mortality rate as high as 70%. Simply put, they met no resistance.

Yellow Fever

The name "yellow fever" refers to the hue of the skin. Other symptoms of yellow fever include yellowed skin, a severe fever, and bloody vomiting. Many individuals perished as a result of this outbreak.

For America 1793, was a dreadful time of year.

Cholera

Although a particularly severe outbreak of a different variety of cholera claimed the lives of some 150,000 Americans in the 1850s, this particular strain had not yet been seen in North America.

Spanish Flu

One of the deadliest pandemics hit a large portion of the world right after World War 1.

This pandemic, often known as the Spanish Flu Epidemic, affected places that had already been devastated by war. Within a short period of time, the United States saw more than 675,000 deaths.

Worldwide, more than 20 million people passed away. In this pandemic, many young, healthy people also perished, in addition to the elderly.

Polio

Polio, a viral illness, affected the nervous system of President Franklin Delano Roosevelt. The 1940s and 1950s saw the disease's impact peak, with catastrophic outbreaks that seemed to spread from city to city. Towns were placed under quarantine.

The peak outbreak came in 1952, when there were 58,000 cases and 3,145 fatalities. Although polio has not been recorded since 1979, it serves as an example of the effects a pandemic can have.

Thanks to Jonas Salk and his work on the polio vaccine

AIDS/HIV

The HIV/AIDS virus was originally identified in 1981. This sickness has been around for a while and has had severe effects. In terms of mortality, AIDS is still the sixth-deadliest illness in North America. Ages 25 to 44 make up the majority of casualties.

The AIDS virus was once thought to be a sexually transmitted illness, but it is now known to travel through needles and from the mother to the fetus. AIDS has been linked to blood transfusions, and solutions have been developed to address this issue.

Tips to avoid:

Door handles in public buildings can spread contagion. Everybody knows that handles in grocery carts are a way to pick up a virus.

Wash your hands; soap and water will kill the majority of germs. Don't touch your face or nose; learn to scratch your nose or face with your elbows. If you are going to cough, do it into your elbow. Just use a surgical mask.

Most respiratory diseases spread through facial touching. A great idea is also to avoid crowds, lines, and places where a lot of people get together. Avoid air travel during periods of epidemics. Many people sitting together for hours and breathing the same air is not a healthy thing to do.

Avoid touching your eyes, nose, and mouth. A hand touches many surfaces and can pick up viruses. Once you touch your eyes, nose, or mouth with contaminated hands, you can transfer the virus to your body.

The possibility of a pandemic outbreak is always there; it has happened and will probably happen again in the near future.

There comes a point in your life when you need to stop reading others people's books and write your own.
Albert Einstein

Lesson 2
Bug in vs bug out-only two choices

Bug out is a military term that is used by preppers to refer to a time when you need to leave your house due to a dangerous situation. Bugging in means sheltering in place-home-while bugging out means leaving your home.

If there is a complete collapse, you have to prepare to deal with a city with no government or local police authority. Communication with other towns and cities is lost; heat and electricity may be gone, or at the very least, food sources will be a problem.

You wouldn't be able to call for emergency services; no ambulance would come for you; no police response would save you if you were attacked; and firefighters wouldn't answer your calls anymore.

You wouldn't get any news of what is happening, and you probably wouldn't know if the disaster has affected other countries around the world.

Can you defend yourself and your family? People may be taken to the streets looking for gas or food; the streets may be full of people walking with guns, stealing, or doing harm to people. No law enforcement, no public services, no supply chain, and money may not be valuable.

Nobody knows how people are going to react, but most of us know what the catastrophe is going to be.

Most people have never survived a major catastrophe or natural disaster, and global supplies are already facing some problems due to many different difficulties.

Even if the United States stays on as a great power, it cannot protect its security alone.

What is concreate jungle?

A concrete jungle is any large, crowded city or urban area with little nature-green areas.

The first day will be rampant crime and looting; there will also be some rapes, and some people will be beaten. Chaos will turn fast in a few hours, especially days into SHTF.

You or a family member could have an injury. The biggest killer is a situation of panic. Panic can cause desperation. You must have a plan for what to do.

The reality is that not everyone has the luxury of heading out for a wilderness farm or a cabin retreat.

The problem with most bug-out plans is that you don't have a destination.

Where are you bugging out?

Do you think the national forest or mountains are going to be solely for you and your family? You believe you just set up a shelter or tent and start hunting for food?

Probably there will be hundreds of hunters hunting, and soon the game will be depleted.

Think this again: You really believe, you just get there and set up your camp? And start hunting or fishing for food without anybody reaching out to you and assaulting you?

I'm sure you will be facing hundreds of hunters hunting and fishing and soon the situation will become catastrophic.

Bugging out is a complex, dangerous and difficult decision.

In the wilderness you will be responsible for your wife, daughters and kids, are you prepared to keep them safe from gangs or thugs trying to take them away?

The biggest obstacle is going to be the city citizen; mass confusion will be full of panic, grocery stores will be looted, and gas stations will be jam-packed lines, fights, and a total disaster.

You will need to carry a lot of fuel to make it to your destination, and find a clear road that can handle the size of your vehicle or truck.

Also, keep in mind that you may need to take a second, third, or fourth route because many routes will be impossible to drive under the circumstances.

Many people believe the National Guard will cordon off the road and block roads, putting a stop to your plans to bulge out. Of course, this will depend on the magnitude of the disaster.

Many disaster books are about leaving from the city. If things have deteriorated and society is unable to uphold the rule of law, only the strong will prevail.

The decision to shelter in place or to leave is complete under many circumstances.

Escapes

You are going to face armed mobs and ambushes. Do you think it is going to be easy to pass by mobs?

It may be crucial, if you are making plans to bug out, to cautiously weigh all alternatives before leaving the protection of your home.

The majority of people do not have the physical ability to bug out, especially if they have to go out on foot.

Do you have the skills to take care of someone, if they get sick or injured? Bugging out could be very challenging for children and pregnant women.

What about if you are in a wheelchair or a big family? This could be a huge, disaster mistake.

The environment will be unfamiliar, and danger will lurk around every corner. Where will you go? Do you have the option of going to another home, cabin, or retreat? How many are in your family? Is there anybody sick who can't walk? Injured?

What about short- or long-term medical conditions? Bugging out means you are on your own. Or someone in your family is blind? Or some elderly people with you.

Lurking danger will be everywhere. Where will you and your family sleep? Where is your next meal coming from? You may have carried food with you for a couple of days. Where can you get drinking water?

Bugging out will create extensive stress.

Preppers use SHTF as a noun for the Apocalypse. After reading many books about SHTF, they all seem to advise leaving the city. To me, this is crazy. Leaving the city is no small feat.

There will be panic, mass confusion, traffic, many people leaving by foot, motorcycles, and bikes, and possibly roadblocks.

I believe it will be almost impossible, but also very dangerous, with gangs and armed people trying to take your car, truck, or anything you have.

Gangs will thrive by taking resources from others. They will roam the city, raping, stealing, and hurting people to meet their desires. You will have only two options: hide or fight and confront them. They will be ruthless and armed; it will be better to avoid them and hide.

In the aftermath of Katrina, drivers were targeted by looters and carjackers. Have you ever studied the exit route that will get you out of your city in a catastrophe? I bet you have not.

The street will probably be blocked by all kinds of vehicles left behind by people who abandon them in panic, run out of gas, or even assault and kill them. People will run to the grocery stores, and everything will sell out quickly. The real problem will begin after a few days, and disaster will reach a very difficult time.

If you are planning to bug out, traveling from point A to point B in a collapsed world without laws will be very difficult and dangerous. Knowing how and where you will travel is a very significant factor.

If you somehow lost your ride and have to walk, try to keep your destination to a five-day total distance of about 10 miles a day; believe me, that's a lot. Your location should be no more than 40 miles from your takeoff-location.

I believe the better option is to hunker down, defend your home, and wait it out.

Misinformation: There is going to be a lot of misinformation, from mouth to mouth or even on the internet if it is still working for a few hours after the collapse. Pay attention to what you hear or read, and verify everything.

Keep your guard up; don't trust anyone who offers you help during a time of crisis. Don't rely on the government for help. Don't trust anyone in a crisis like this.

Who are the daydream planners?

These are preppers who believe that they can survive by living off the land, hunting, and doing some farming, and surviving through the apocalypse. This fantasy planner ignores reality; most of them have never done any of these activities.

In reality, there are few people who understand what it is really like to survive in the wilderness or to live in the streets, park, or under a bridge. The idea of bugging out into the wilderness like many books suggest is not a realistic perspective; one thing is going camping or hunting for a few days, to live for months or years in the wildness.

Weather and climate: You need to think of regional considerations: Climate where you live: cold, hot, humid, like Florida, where I live warm, mosquitoes, wild animals, rain, hurricanes.

Remember, no matter what, you will all be fighting for your basic needs to survive. Sometimes the only option is to escape by foot. Avoid the major avenues and streets likely to be congested. Encounters with others might turn hostile.

Your car may breakdown, you might have to abandon it, and you will be walking.

You turn a corner, and you are face-to-face with a mob setting fires and attacking people. What are you going to do? Are you ready for what's next?

Other issues include the fact that if your spouse or kids start to panic, the escape or evacuation will become a nightmare.

Bugging out danger

People will be desperate for food and gas for their car or truck.

Injured: If you get hurt, your bugging plans are done.

Benefits of bugging in

If a terrible disaster happens and you hunker down at home, you have time to check how the city and surrounding area are doing.

The majority of situations are best faced in a well-prepared and stocked home.

Your homes provide you with a safe shelter from the sun, wind, rain, and snow even when the power fails; a plus is that you are familiar with your surroundings. Even if your home is damaged, I'm 100% sure it will be a better option than becoming a street walker with no place to go and looking for a place to stay the night.

The majority of scenarios can be best faced from the safety of your home.

Your home is the best choice because:

That's where all your supplies are.

It is impossible to bring as many supplies on the road as you have at home.

You know your neighborhood.

You know the escape routes.

You can tell quickly if there is an unfamiliar person walking around.

It's less complicated to discover protection in numbers. It's important to make a group work together to survive. A group is also necessary for safety against invaders, gangs, and crazy individuals.

It is estimated that 83% of the U.S. population lives in urban areas in 2024.

An urban community is one that's in a city or town; many people live there, and there are lots of different varieties of buildings close to each other. A suburb is a location where individuals live just outside of a city or town. Suburbs are smaller urban neighborhoods that border cities.

The suburbs are made up mostly of single-family homes, stores, and services.

When a collapse occurs, if you live in the city, the power will be cut off. No more refrigerators, lights, the ability to communicate, or cooking. For those with health issues such as diabetes that require refrigeration to keep medicine and other people with medicine requirements, the situation will become a nightmare.

What is urban survival?

The benefits of facing danger from your home outweigh the idea of bugging out, unless the situation at home demands it. Defense and security are much easier with your familiar home steps; you also have a good idea of your neighbors.

Situations to bug out:

Imminent home danger
Civil riots reach your home.
Being on the road makes you and your family an easier target.

Medical issues-anything-could make you sick and leave you groggy and unable to drive or make decisions. What about if you get injured?

Bug out shelter list:

Tarp	Shed
Cabin	RV or camp
Three houses	Trailer

Examples of reason to leave home:

Category hurricane 5

Natural disaster that made your home unsafe

Flooded home

Burn home down

Civil unrest and the mob is already looting homes a block from your home.

If you decide to bug out here are some suggestions

Avoid open places, new roads
Disguise your bug out shelter with natural materials
Camouflage vehicle, tent or shelter
Use materials that blend in
Use flat paint to reduce glare to blend with the surrounding
Avoids shiny colors

One irrational thing I always hear is that if anything happens, I'm bugging out to the woods. This is so unfeasible; it is ridiculous and is also irresponsible. Thousands of people are thinking the same as you. How many days of people hunting will it take before the deer, rabbits, and squirrels in your area are completely hunted out?

Think about it: even if you own your land, you are going to find people setting up tents. If they are going to live and hunt on your land, how are you going to stop them? Are you ready to fight, maybe kill, or be killed to stop them? Every minute of the day and night will be a struggle in many different ways.

Everglades-Tropical weather

Some books and people in my state of Florida suggest bugging out to the Florida Everglades. Based on my experience, conversations with experts in the Everglades, and reading dozens of articles about the Everglades, I've concluded that this is not a place to bug out. I have hunted deep in the Everglades for years, and I'm sure it won't be an easy task to survive months after months or even a year in there.

You may be experiencing excessive temperatures, heavy rainfall, and frequent thunder and lightning. Violent storms arise generally closer to the end of the summer months. Hurricanes, tropical rain, sun, and bugs are normal. Bacteria carrying mosquitoes and other insects are immediate dangers. You must protect yourself against bites in the tropics. For bites within the tropics, even the smallest scratch can quickly emerge as dangerously infected. Rapidly cure any injury, even if it is small.

The author hunting

Cold is a dangerous enemy; it numbs the mind and body, and if intense, it could kill you. Wind chill increases the hazards in cold weather. Unless you have experience camping in the wild in a tent, not in an AV with a shower, air conditioning, and a small kitchen, you don't have the slightest idea how hard it will be to survive in a situation where there is no food, no shelter, and no protection.

Hunting is a big challenge, especially if you are not an experienced hunter. Fishing is easy; the only problem is the water quality where the fish are caught. On a summer day in the Everglades, the heat, humidity, and mosquitoes are irresistible.

According to the Mayo Clinic, there are three heat-related syndromes: heat cramps, heat exhaustion, and heatstroke, which are the most severe. Causes of heat exhaustion include exposure to high temperatures, especially when combined with high humidity and strenuous physical activity.

Heatstroke calls for an emergency remedy. Untreated heatstroke can quickly harm your brain, heart, kidneys, and muscles. Heatstroke causes more death in American cities than all other weather events combined. In warmer settings with snakes and insects, don't stick your hands, feet in any holes you can't see in.

Bug in

A house, a shelter has been a source of protection and comfort as human kind can remember.

You have protection from rain, snow, cold, wild animals, storms and assault if you are in the lookout.

You have stocked guns, ammo, you also fortified your doors and windows, and you are ready to defend against rioters, gangs, and home invasion. In a collapse there will not be rule of law, inmates will escape from jail, moral less, horny, criminal and rapist will be everywhere, wives, and daughters will be in the greatest danger.

If you plan to stay put, be ready to be a bad-ass and to fight day, night and day.

The power Grid

The U.S. electrical grid is vulnerable to disruption. Long-term electrical grid down situation. If the power grid fails baby foods, formula, canned foods, cigarettes, beer, ammunition would be the first items to disappear.

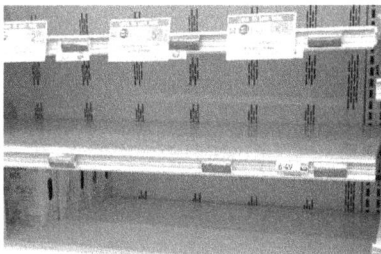

Special Situations

After one month after the grid down scenery. Stores will be depleted from food; in general all supply will be gone. People who weren't ready will start starvation. There are little doubts a total collapse will make urban living almost impossible to survive.

The gangs are going to be roaming the streets looking for essay victims. This means you not only have to be able to defend yourself but also how to defend yourself and your family.

The city will be very dangerous in the initial months.

Thousands of people will be hungry, and will organize mass violence, mugging each other for food, and medicine.

Most of those surviving mostly by taking from others.

You don't think this could happen? Go and read and learn what happened throughout Los Angeles riots or after Katrina in New Orleans.

Urban threes will be gone; in winter, people will need firewood for heat. The first place to get it is in your own backyard. Next up will be public trees and park trees. In a few years, there may be no more threes in the urban city for people to cut and use.

Backyard gardens will become popular out of necessity; another possible problem with your backyard garden will be neighbors' requests.

The best way is to remain hidden in an urban environment, and heavily fortified home or building, better if it has a hidden or obscure entrance.

You may need to construct or set-up some fighting positions to watch safe like a shed, barricade, tower, house three or ditch to defend your home.

Remember anything fortified build can be used against your house by an opponent.

Risks in the city:

The city poses some severe risks during a crisis. The four most serious ones are:

1. The disintegrate of social order (riots),

2. The failure of the water treatment and delivery systems,

3. The depletion of food supplies and

4. The failure of the power grid.

Waste neighborhood

When there won't be indoor plumbing or waste pick-up services, neighborhoods are going to stink. They will dump their waste down the street somewhere in the middle of the night. It will just sit there in the sun, rain, and wind, and rodents will plunge in.

The urban city where you live will become pretty unpleasant; rotting bodies' odor will fill the air; unfed pet dogs have progressively formed hostile packs.

The road will be terrible.

Roads will be impossible to drive through; for a few years, roads and bridges will be okay, but without maintenance, they will quickly begin to collapse. Potholes will get bigger and bigger, and bridges will deteriorate and finally fail.

Industrial skills

Sewing, mending clothes, and resoling shoes and boots will become necessary crafts. Also, carpentry might, for sure, become useful. You may be able to use those skills to barter or trade with neighbors.

Body hair

Shaving every day will become a goal from the past. Most survivalists won't want to waste time and energy. Men will probably have more beard, and women will have unshaven legs and armpits.

Weather planning

The weather for the days of the week will be a total surprise; you'll know the general seasons. However, you won't know what the next day is bringing.

You don't know if the days are going to bring storms, droughts, or snow. Because weather forecasting will no longer operate.

Weekend vanish

The whole idea of a weekend will vanish. When surviving is your only concern, you don't readily get any days off.

Do you remember the saying? Thank God it's Friday. Sound familiar?

No morning coffee

Coffee shops will no longer operate. Maybe you have left a few grounds that you stockpile, but how long would you have for a long haul? Coffee beans will become a scarce treat, not often found, and valuable if you do.

Make-up, fragrance, and hair care products

Make-up, perfume, and hair shampoo will be rare to find if you haven't shaved in many days. Who will like to get dressed up?

Families live closer.

Families will stick together because these will be the only humans they can trust.

Alcohol Kept

Alcohol may be saved for sanitizing essentials and cleansing wounds; consequently, even as drug and alcohol abuse will no longer be eliminated, it's not going to be day-to-day use.

Digital photos

Photos stored on a laptop or in the cloud will not be possible to open. On the other hand, physical photos will turn out to be precious for families. They will have incalculable personal value.

No more political parties—no national elections

Elections might be an issue of the past. It is possible that after many months or years, a local leader will try to be chosen through small elections to try to govern some local towns or city subs.

The paper dollar after the Teotwawki will only be useful to make a fire or use as toilet paper.

Adaptation is the key to survival

The enemy is anybody who's going to get you killed, no matter which side he is on.

Joseph Heller

Lesson Home 3
The problems of living in an urban environment when SHTF

Water problems: A major issue that you will face is securing drinkable water. Also, water, which you can use for washing and preparing food and for cleaning yourself and your family, the city's pipes and water facilities, will likely cease to function when a collapse happens.

After three weeks everybody will be aggressive looking for drinkable water, no matter how much they can get.

You have plenty of time to prepare your home for a disaster; it should include the presence of an intruder, entry gates, fences, natural alarms, and window and door reinforcement. If your home is difficult to penetrate, looters might walk past your house.

Homeowners will no longer maintain their homes, which will begin to deteriorate a few days after the SHTF. After a few years, most homes will be run down, especially the abandoned ones.

No more mowed lawns; weeds will grow out of control. Cracks will be in roads, sidewalks, and abandoned gardens. Think for a moment about this dreadful situation. As soon as winter hits, individuals will need firewood for heat.

Backyard and urban three will soon be gone. In a few years, there may be no more or just a few urban threes.

Pets

Once food turns out to be insufficient, People will have a hard time feeding their pets or finding time to take care of them.

Don't have obvious defenses; an obvious defense makes it look like you've got something in your home that is worth guarding.

You must carry a weapon at all times when you're working outside your home; the devil doesn't wait until nightfall to attack.

Try to be invisible to looters and thugs.

Keep the sounds of tools and engines to a minimum.

It smells like wood and smoke from cooking.

Protect your castle with force if you have to, but only in the most critical circumstances and as a last resort.

Once a gang finds you, they are going to have you scouted. They will like to find out things like:

How many people are with you at home?

How many weapons and types do you have?

How many defenders are there?

Who is in charge?

Does your group have any patrols or times to do patrolling?

If you have a second-floor bedroom, you need a flexible ladder in your home, and you should practice using it once a year if possible. Also, for safety reasons, you must sleep downstairs so you can hear any noise better. This will give you a better time to react. Sleep in an inside room, which provides you with greater protection from gunfire and rocks.

Backyard pools won't be used for fun, but the good thing about a backyard pool in a STTF disaster is that you have an entire tank full of life-saving survival water.

Here you have a problem situation; probably your neighbors want to share the water, or maybe strangers will also like to take your water. What are you going to do? Are you prepared to shoot intruders?

A pool is one of the best survival blessings, but it could turn into a nightmare.

Prepared for a SHTF are three requirements.

Perimeter:

Distinctive areas outside your home property

Barriers:

Obstructions that you put up on the exterior of your home to prevent intruders from entering.

Fortified:

The interior of your home

Neighborhood security

Neighborhood defense would be vital in a SHTF situation because there is power in numbers. The more people participating, the more effective the complete security will be.

In a post-SHTF situation, the main entrance streets to a neighborhood could be blocked by abandoned cars and old furniture to stop gangs and thugs from gaining entrance.

The people in the neighborhood could help take turns as security watch; have some volunteer snipers on roofs, ready to defend the neighborhood. With an adequate number of personal, not only can you have a rotation of assignments to support 24 hours, but you can also have guards watch nights and days.

Could this stop gangs and thugs from entering the neighborhood? Probably not, but it will stop them from gaining free entrance. If they came in motorcycles or pickup trucks, they would think twice about living in their vehicle, searching homes by foot, and being open to gunfire from unfamiliar roof tops.

Probably they will leave and look for an easy neighborhood to loot. Probably later in the month, they are going to be back. For now, the neighborhood is safe.

The only bad thing is that as the situation gets worse, you may also find a need to protect yourself and your family from those within.

Experts in the subject claim it is better to be a lone wolf than not. It depends on you, your neighborhood, and your situation.

If you want to go alone

The sequence of threes gives you a guide on how to organize fundamental survival skills: first shelter, then water, and finally food.

You must keep in mind and be prepared to face physical and mental challenges, such as dealing with the lack of sleep, coping with obtaining water and making sure it is safe to drink, obtaining food for the family, and safeguarding your home.

All this stress is going to take a huge toll not only on your body but also on everybody in your home.

If you want to go alone, you must adhere to extraordinary safety precautions. If you and your group go out scouting or bartering, you must be sure nobody follows you back home.

You should not keep a bicycle or motorcycle in front of your home at any time. A night makes sure there is no light visible from the outside; if you have one, make sure it is only a soft candlelight. This way, you can be just like the surrounding homes.

Also, when you cook, if you have the provisions to do it, make sure to incorporate at least three or four days in between so gangs can't track the smell back to your home. Same with smoke; you can see smoke blocks away, no noise, no generator for hours, and make sure to alternate days to use it.

If you have chickens, keep them as far from the front of your home as you can. Place a wood barrier and a curtain on the side of the cage facing your home to diminish noise.

If you talk on your walkie-talkie or ham radio, keep it as short as possible so thieves and gangs can't track you. Finally, your wife and daughters should try not to be in the front garden.

If they need to do some chores or garden, have them wear big pants, wear their hair up, and wear a hat or cap so people can't tell there is a woman from afar.

They must keep their eyes open while doing chores in front of the house. If they see somebody approaching unknown in the neighborhood, they should immediately get inside before the intruder or intruders' lookouts get close to them to identify them as women.

We know this is going to be a gloomy, dark, violent, and overwhelming dangerous period, but if you want to go it alone, it has to be done for safety reasons at least for the first year. You must wait until things get a little bit more normal or the situation gets more controlled.

According to experts, if you follow these recommendations, maybe it will be OK. Why are the thugs going to pick your house to attack out of the thousands of houses in your neighborhood?

Fortifying the home from inside

The harder you make it for the aggressors to attack you and invade your home or apartment, the better chance you have of surviving the attack.

The basic wood panel provides an exceptional barrier against an intruder; the bad is that it takes away from you the ability to visually monitor it outside your home.

There is nothing worse than hearing a noise outside and not being able to see what it is. You can fix this by making a kind of opening, like a peephole.

Lock down access points and nail your studs collectively in lengthwise pairs at ninety angles to shape braces. Hammering brasses horizontally across every door Use longer nails and leave a few inches of the nails protruding for a clean removal later on.

The first thing you must do is fortify your home.

If the power is out, keep your house as dark as possible; you don't want to attract attention. Powering your home could be a hard and dangerous process, and cooking and heating your home will be very hard after utilities are shut down. Even if you have a low-burning stove, soon you will run out of fuel. Always be aware of the risk of carbon monoxide poisoning if you cook inside.

During a long-term disaster, the water will sooner or later stop running, and you won't be able to flush your toilet.

Night camouflage: it could be dark, but you have to take precautions so you won't attract attention.

Move at night in the shadows as much as possible.

Keep the noise down, especially in the city.

No fire or cooking; cooking will help create smells; be careful.

If your home is your first priority for shelter and has been partially destroyed or shattered, use cardboard to insulate yourself from the ground. Use blankets and pillows to build a shelter inside your home. It should be as low to the ground as possible.

Another great strategy is that if you live in a two-story home, an elevated position with a nice 360-degree view will be great; being high above the ground provides a huge tactical advantage.

Some items are needed to secure a home and property.

A plywood window or door is a two-person job. The recommended thickness should be 1/2" for window openings, 5/8" for door openings, and 34" for sliding door and French door openings. Keep in mind that thugs can enter through a second-floor window

Some items you need to protect your windows are:

Plywood

2x4s

Hand saws,

Tools: multi-tools (knife, axe, hatchet)

Hammers, screw drivers, and pliers

Rope

Measuring tape

Fortify your perimeter

There are two different approaches to recommendations from specialists. One is to make your home look deserted and dirty, with empty boxes and old cloth on the front porch, making you believe that looters have been there. The other is keeping your home normal, like people are living there.

The problem with the first one is that some team, gang, or bandit may choose your home to break into and take it as a shelter for them. The second option problem is that gangs, mobs, and bandits know there has to be supplies inside, whether it's women or daughters. Both are very dangerous options.

You have to decide which option is better suited for you, your family, and your neighborhood. I personally believe that somewhere in between is the better option.

Consider making your home less desirable by throwing random junk on the lawn. You could line old cars, buses, or trucks around your protection zone. The problem with this idea is that you are telling people where you are. Make it appear as if it has been ransacked.

Many preppers recommend building a very tall fence. To me, this will make it obvious that you have stuff worth stealing. If you are planning to build a fence, make it as innocent as possible so you don't draw attention to your house.

The objective is to keep people from getting close to your home.

Creating a defensive perimeter around your house is the best way to keep attackers as far away as possible.

Untrained people will be noisy as they walk as a group. Probably they don't have any training, so they will take a head-on attack to the front of your home. If you defend your home, they will probably leave and look for an easier target.

The attack could last several days. During this time, you need supplies inside your home, not outside in the shed or garage. If you make a tough target, the looters will move to look for an easier target.

Here are the most important items to have close by:

Water	First aid kit
Food	Weapons
Medicine	Bullets

Fire prevention supplies:

Gas masks: an attacking mob could use propane or insecticide to try to get you out.

Fire smoke

The best thing you can do is obtain a supply of N95 masks. N95 masks are built to U.S. specs. KN96 masks are built to Chinese specs.

Most of the people who survived a revolution were the ones who hid, lied low, and waited for the right moment to come out of the shadows.

Home security 24/7

You have to make up a schedule for patrolling your property for 24 hours.

Create a watch rotation; you need to have someone always patrolling your perimeter from two to four hours at a time.

There may be a family member or one of your teammates taking alternative guard time. Set up a guard tower, a second-floor balcony, the top of a truck, or build one so your property can be seen. Make sure that a thug can't sneak on you or a long-range rifle can't hit you.

Nighttime

Times will be dangerous, especially at night; you should plan on sleeping in shifts to keep watch. When the lights go out, looters and criminals come out to attack.

Daylight is better reserved for resting, working around, or in your home. Darkness becomes very dangerous in SHTF circumstances. Stay inside at night; going out at night is going to be very dangerous in a grid-down situation especially when you are asleep.

You must make sure someone stays every night watching; your family or group should watch on alternative days or hours. Keep weapons within reach at all times. You need people to help you do work, to take care of you when you're sick or hurt, or to watch your back when you are sleeping or doing the innumerable tasks that you will be occupied with after a major disaster.

Tarp the lights from candles or lanterns; you don't want to become a beacon to the thieves or mob. If you need to use a light, always use a red light; a white light will draw others to you. If you have a home that is lit in a world of darkness, you will for sure have visitors.

Two-way radios have been a dependable mode of communication in the concrete jungle. You need one that can work well, whether it is close or long-range communication. The best frequency to use in this setting has to be UHF.

Dogs

Dogs are an incredible help in a STHF situation; they are loud and better than any alarm system. The problem with dogs is that if your dog is not capable of keeping quiet in a dangerous situation, you will have your location exposed all the time. If you are lost in the woods or trapped in a vehicle in the cold, your dog can help you keep warm by snuggling with you on a cold night.

Barbed wire rolls

Barbed wire is a metal mesh used to prevent the passage of animals and humans. Many places have laws that prevent people from installing barbed wire in front of their homes. It is great to have these barbed wire rolls in your shed in an SHTF situation.

There will be no law restrictions then.

You can also place spikes or glass pieces on top of your fence to keep intruders from climbing it. Of course, the barbed wire fence can be cut, but it will slow them down, delaying an attack and giving you more time to get ready.

In a middle-class neighborhood, most front houses only have 12 to 18 feet from the sidewalk to the home. So the idea of installing barbed wire is out of the question. Why all that work and the cost? Your home will look out of place and will attract attention right away. You don't want this.

I think it will be better just to make it look undesirable with old boxes and clothes rags everywhere and an old, dirty, broken sofa or chairs in front. The grass is uncut, and the windows are boarded with wood.

So the mob or gangs find it less appealing and keep walking down the neighborhood looking for a more appealing home to break into and steal.

Chain link

Probably it won't give you concealment, but it will slow down people.

Clearing Sight-lines

Don't have anything so the attackers can't hide behind it. I recommend fences that don't obstruct your view.

Having some clear distance between your fence and your home gives you the opportunity to react and get a plan going.

Effective

No tree obstructing view of driveway home

Nothing of value noticeable from the street.

Wire fence if the home front is adequate

Flaws

A short fence with no view of the property boundary

No security watching the home perimeter

Sex slave prisoners

Gangs will have no hesitation in looting or robbing anyone they see; they will have no problem breaking into your home and taking anything they want by force. As distasteful as it sounds, that will include female members in your household who run the risk of being raped and taken as sex slave prisoners.

Booby Traps

You need to do whatever you have to do to keep you and your family safe. Having an alarm will alert you when someone enters your home security perimeter and give you time to get ready to defend yourself.

These are devices to catch animals or people by surprise. Is it legal? In a world that collapses, there won't be any laws, so you don't have to worry about whether something is legal or not.

Your booby trap should blend with your setting. If not, it won't take long for an invader to notice and bypass them. Make certain to camouflage them. Set up booby traps outside your home perimeter, ranging from harmless to more deadly.

You don't want to install man-trapping devices, like spiked pits, etc.; they take a lot of work. You run the risk of hurting yourself or your kids, especially in an emergency attack when you and your team members are occupied.

The danger is getting yourself hurt by the things that were meant to protect you. You must think that if you have younger kids, it is better to go with a less-lethal defense booby trap.

The Tripwire Trap is an easy classic trap. It is a wire that extends across a pathway, like from a tree to a door frame or similar object.It's better to use braided fishing line because it's almost impossible to see, plus it won't split if a person walks through it.

Tin can alarm

Materials:

Aluminum cans-Fishing line-wire or Paracord-Pebbles-small rocks

You can use several tin cans and a fishing line or something comparable; you can generate enough noise to shock intruders and at the same time alert you to their presence. Place some small rocks inside each can or anything else that clanks, and tie about ten or more cans together, or more depending on the space you want to cover. Use the fishing line or Paracord to secure a loop around two trunks.

When a trespasser's legs get caught on the tripwire, the trigger will make the tin cars move or fall and make a very loud noise. You can place this alarm in front of your door, back door, by the fence or an nearby three.

You must keep in mind that setting traps is, at this time, against the law. If you hurt someone with a trap, even if they are breaking into your home, you will be liable for prosecution. You could also injure yourself or a family member.

Front doors

You must protect your front door—with wood pieces, metal bars, or whatever you can. Heavy furniture will give you some protection behind the doors.

Sliding doors

They are very dangerous and an easy entryway. You must cover them with wood panels. Consider double-paned glass or glass with embedded wire to ensure your glass back door security. You also can place a dowel rod to ensure your glass back door security. A dowel rod is a cylindrical stick and is used to insert the track of sliding glass door, thugs can't open the door with the dowel rod holding it shut.

Windows bar

Sure, they can protect your home, but the downside is that it makes a fire emergency extremely difficult.

Windows

You must protect them with wood panels, or shutters, especially on the lowest floor and basement windows. If possible, set up sandbags and books behind windows in case the aggressors shoot at your home. Screening your house windows with chicken wire reduces the risk of the mob burning your house with a Molotov cocktail.

Garage doors

The garage door is an easy entry point. You must protect the garage door with wood or chain, or you may park an old car and chain the door to the car. Garage doors are a potentially weak spot in your home.

You can also use a heavy steel bar attached horizontally and vertically to the inside frame in the back of the door; you can also use a wood panel. Anything to make it protected and difficult to break.

Designate a safe room for fire.

It's crucial to have a room so your family can retreat during an attack. If the invaders get frustrated and angry because they were not able to enter and take your home, they may set your house on fire.

You must make a point to have some fire extinguishers in different parts of your house, make sure they work, and teach every member how to use them.

Also, keep some heavy blankets and buckets of sand ready for this situation if it ever happens. Never use water to put out a Molotov cocktail; it will help the flame spread. You must also have a secret escape passage in case you have to exit because of the fire.

This could be to your back shed or through a back fence gate if your back fence is high, made of wood or blocks. Have some heavy boxes or an old ladder so your group can use it to escape. Where are you going to escape? To a family member close by? A friend's house?

Make sure to have discussed this with your team members and family group. This is the worst situation that could happen during an attack.

In addition, if there are many attackers committing to breaking, it will be impossible to hold off the attack, and they will likely succeed. Any house can be broken into if the invaders have enough time to attack when they know no police or help will be coming.

I hope nothing like this ever happens, but being prepared is an SHTF scenario.

Make sure to remove or hide flammable materials from the exterior of your home so the mobs don't have easy access to them.

Class A fires: paper, cloth, wood, and plastic

Class B fires: flammable liquids, oil, gasoline, and kerosene

Class C fires: electrical equipment, wiring, and motors

Class D fires: combustible metals, aluminum, and titanium

How to extinguish burning clothes:

Running will cause you to inhale harmless gases and spread the fire to other parts of your body.

If you have a blanket or heavy wool blanket, wrap it around yourself, patting at the flames.

Cover your face with the ground.

Drop to the ground and roll over repeatedly.

Treat the burn areas with cool water; do not break blisters or disturb charred skin. Wrap burn areas loosely in dry, sterile bandages.

If you are ready and defend yourself, they may leave and look for an easy home to break, especially if they are only eight or ten untrained guys.

They don't want to get hurt or killed; they just want an easy, targeted home.

Window air conditioners are a target.

A unit hanging out of a window usually means that in many cases, the only thing the crowd has to do is push the unit inward, and they are in. So you must somehow secure these units or close them for God's sake with wood or metal. Anyway, there is no electricity.

Hedges and shrubs

There are many natural barriers you can use to fortify your property. Of course, you have to keep in mind the climate you live in. You don't want your plants to conceal the attackers. Make sure your hedges won't block your view of intruders.

Here are some defensive plants you can use:

Century plant	Barberry
Spanish bayonet	Wild Blackberry
Firethorn	

Backyard Livestock-gardening

You also have to keep your vegetable garden out of view. If you have backyard livestock, you must come up with a plan to protect them. Animals and gardens need to be away from sightings from the street, and if you have livestock, it is important that the noises be far away from people walking by.

Solar panel systems will be in high demand. The difficulty with solar panels is that they are complicated to hide, and this will surely attract looters.

Blocking your driveway and your street

You can block your driveway and the street in front of your house so no vehicles go through. The downside of this is that you would be blocking your own escape.

Gangs will have no hesitation in looting or robbing anyone they see; they will have no problem breaking into your home and taking anything they want by force. As distasteful as it sounds, that will include female members in your household who run the risk of being raped and taken as sex slave prisoners.

Elderly relatives, young, nice-looking women, wives, and daughters will be in the greatest danger.

The cheapest way is to make a homemade spike trap with a nail or screw, typically through a piece of wood. When positioned correctly, it can slow down or stop a vehicle from reaching your home.

This trap can be dangerous because, in an emergency getaway for you and your family, it could disable your car, truck, or motorcycle.

If you get your water from a well or a stream close to your home, you need to bury your waste at least 250 feet downstream from your water source. As you must know, it is dangerous to drink contaminated water from feces, as it can give you all kinds of diseases and infections; the most common one is E. coli.

What to expect in a SHTF situation in an urban setting

In fact, an SHTF situation in the middle of a city is going to be one of the most panic-stricken places you ever find yourself in.

Looting only takes place in retail stores, malls, and businesses, and rarely in homes. Home looting will take place during long, extensive periods of extreme disaster.

Looting goes hand in hand with rioting when people take advantage of mass hysteria and confusion for their personal gain.

Martial Law

In a situation of great crisis, some or all of these measures will be taken. Martial law has been used in a limited way in the United States, such as in the New Orleans Battle of New Orleans, the great Chicago fire of 1871, the 1906 San Francisco earthquake, the Omaha race riot of 1919, or the Lexington riots.

Also, Lincoln issued a martial law order on April 1, 1861, allowing the army to arrest and detain without trial those considered disloyal.

Curfew before or after dark, no doubt a curfew will be imposed. This has actually happened in a number of cities across the US.

What is martial law?

Martial law is the military imposition of control over normal civil functions by the government. Probably the military will do a random house search to find our firearms and supplies hidden, so keep your firearms and supplies hidden.

Hide some weapons to protect from searchers and confiscation. Offer a deceive gun to authorities if pressured. Have a story plan like you lost, or got stolen, if they know and ask you for other weapons,

There are only three choices you can do under Martial Laws

A-fight back—not a great option
B-Go away to the hills, hide and elude the government—easier said than done.

C-Live under the government's rule of law. Dangerous choice.
Under martial law, it is going to take intelligent thinking and keeping cool to survive.

You want to avoid two things during martial law:
Being seen and heard.
If you want to escape martial law, then you would rather bug out to an extremely remote place than bug in.

Detention camps: Some might not want to hear this, but detention camps would clearly be warranted if the situation called for them.

History shows us that those who end up in camps or mass shelters are the least likely to survive.

Blocked roads: Under martial law, you can count on the fact that almost all roads will be blocked by the police, the National Guard, or the army.

Rations: The military will probably be in charge of rationing food, water, and supplies.

Military tribunals: don't expect a standard jury and trial.

If confronted by the military keep your cool and don't make any threats. Leave without you pissing them off. Soldiers may just seize anyone who gives them problems. They may take you to a concentration camp. Your family needs you; be smart. In a time of collapse, there is no telling what drastic event is going to take place.

If they take your gun, keep it cool; you probably have more hidden in your home, or you can obtain one from a friend or exchange one for any supplies you have. In the aftermath of Hurricane Katrina, New Orleans police and the National Guard forcibly seized all civilian firearms from law-abiding citizens.

Martial law under a government with bad intentions can have devastating consequences. Can martial law under a dictatorial government prevail in the U.S.? To the UK, Canada, and other western countries? Don't you think it can happen?

Mass arrest: avoid riots and protests; you don't want to be taken up in a mass arrest.

Law enforcement: If the police or army still operating, you may not have to worry about the bad guys, but are you safe from law enforcement?

Martial law and the media: The government will control the media during martial law. You have to listen, so it will help you know about the new rules, curfew times, and relevant information to adjust your movement.

You can tap into HAM radio frequencies to get information from those who are off the grid. They will be telling the truth. At the time of this writing, U.S. laws require a license to operate a ham radio.

Think about it: in a situation where the government has collapsed, who is going to check on you or go after you to enforce the law?

Stay camouflaged. Stay undercover from a drone or helicopter.

Fear is always there, it's a survival instinct. You must need to know how to manage it.
                                                                    Jimmy Chin

Lesson 4

It is difficult to lose a tracking dog.

Experts claim that losing a trained dog is virtually impossible; eluding a tracking dog can keep you and your family away from a political or concentration camp.

Experts claim one strategy to evade a tracking dog is to escape into a very populated area, like a big city.

This trick, according to the specialists in the subject matter, is overwhelm a dog's senses. You must keep in mind that this route will bring different dangers to you and your family.

If you are in the forest, their advice is to move with the wind. You will need to move downwind; your smell will drift downwind. Another tip is to climb up a cliff or rocky mountaintop; tracking dogs are not rock climbers.

Experts also affirm that it is another trick to set a fire if the wind is blowing in the direction you are fleeing from. The hope is that the smoke and flames will stop and confuse a tracking dog.

By failing to prepare, you are preparing to fail,
Benjamin Franklin

Gray man

The "gray man" theory can be applied to anyone, man or woman, of any age who needs to blend into a crowd in a disastrous situation. The gray man theory is the ability to move through a crowd without drawing attention to yourself.

Going into an area purposefully increases your chances of experiencing violence. The last thing you want is to be standing in any sort of crowd.

You need to blend in, and becoming a gray man allows you to do that. The gray man doesn't stand out. This makes you much less of a target.

The same is true for your backpack. A neutral color, nothing bright, no camouflage—the less obvious, the better for you.

Avoid eye contact with everyone, move as naturally as possible, and it will appear that you are going with the crowd. Confrontation needs to be prevented at any cost. Keep your head down, and if any person appears aggressive, do your best to stay far from him or her.

Don't talk to anyone. However, if you do, be cautious about what you say.

Keep your hair messy and refrain from using anything with a strong smell, like deodorant or perfume.

Travel in groups of at least four people, and be ready to fight with your firearm if you have to.

Make or find a map and be aware of your surroundings. Learn the neighboring area, including streets, as best you can.

Be alert if you are being followed.

Keep your eyes open and change course immediately if you suspect anything is wrong.

Do you appear to be alone? Eliminate the soft target by looking rough and maybe a little crazy. However, the better you blend in, the better, but never look like a soft target.

Take a small backpack big enough to hide supplies, and a short-barreled shotgun. Take smaller streets and avoid taking big avenues to reduce contact with other people, exposing you to fewer hostile confrontations. Scuff your backpack to make it much less desirable.

Stick tape, use duct tape, or do other things to make them look old, poor, and less appealing.

Carry an item or two so you can quickly alternate the way you look. That could be a hat, a different shirt, a wig, or sunglasses.

Camouflage at night

Camouflage at night requires special consideration. Move at night if possible to avoid being seen. Keep to the shadows as much as possible. Keep the conversation and noise down.

Local weather

What temperatures are you going to encounter along your route? Time of year and duration of your excursion. You must take precautions and be ready for the weather.

Alone

You should never make the excursion alone; there is safety in numbers, and of course, groups travel slower.

Tips:

Keeping a low profile keeps you from becoming a target from criminals.

Blending in- blend into your surroundings.

Adaptability-Adjusting fast for any situation that may arise

Clothing and footwear

When you are traveling on foot, you must keep in mind that your group is going to be exposed to the elements. You must cover your arms and legs on any trip through harsh environments, no matter the weather. Mosquitoes are a threat to your health; the fewer exposed areas on your body, the better.

If you are being chased, don't run in a straight line; it will be easier for the groups to shoot you or capture you. If they are shooting at you, run in a zigzag pattern. Judge the path you are taking; if there is a puddle, for example, or pond, how deep is it? Is it worth it?

There are two basic types of hiding spots: cover and concealment. Cover will protect you from physical attacks (baseball, stick, or fist), but you can be seen. Concealment offers no physical protection, but it makes you hard to find.

You can gather foliage to cover yourself with; you can also cover your face with mud. If your clothes are bright, you can cover them with mud too.

Make your stature as low as possible, and try to breathe slowly for a long time.

Try not to move; you don't have to see them as long as you can hear them.

Exit the situation as soon as you can, assess the situation according, and remember that running will attract attention from others.

At these moments, you may not be pursed. According to the circumstances, one should modify one's plans. In battle, there are two attack methods: direct and indirect.

Do not open your bag in a place where others can see what is inside.

Up a three

Climbing a tree is a good option to hide in the woods. Not to many people look up, and most are not taught to do it. Of course, if you get spotted, you don't have any place to escape. This decision depends in the situation.

Bury yourself

This is a clever practice that has been used in the past intensely during wars.

Water bottles reuse

Health advocates advice against reusing bottles made from plastic #1 polyethylene, known as PET or PETE, this includes disposable water bottles, soda and juices bottles.

Studies claim that the plastic used put chemicals toxins in the water. This happens over a long period. In an emergency you need to use anything available. Better than die of thirst right there at the moment.

All good thoughts and ideas mean nothing without action
Mahatma Gandhi

Gray woman

Any woman is going to be more of a target for many reasons in a catastrophic event; this doesn't get addressed enough in books on prepping in an emergency. About half of the population that is going to be affected is going to be women.

I know a woman who can shoot better than me and won't think for a moment about being on guard or duty. Many women would rather be patrolling in the dark than taking care of a garden or cooking.

For safety reasons, there are some things a woman can do to prevent becoming a victim of sexual crimes and violence. She should wear big-size pants and shirts and tennis shoes, not dresses. Clothes not tight to soften or conceal noticeable endowment. No makeup, perfume, or nail polish that sets you apart from a gray man

No jewelry, piercings, rings, purses, woman shoes, woman hats, also wears a short haircut, etc. It is not hard for a woman to look like a gray man from a distance. Looking like a homeless person will help because most people will try to distance themselves from this type of person. This way, a woman has a better chance of hiding her figure. This may help a woman because she can wear all kinds of different clothes.

Stockpiling

You should be stockpiling any time you come across disposable feminine products.

Learn to be alone

If you are a woman alone, roughing it will take on a whole new meaning in a SHTF situation. Coping with that time of the month, sex, birth control, finding food, surviving, and keeping your shelter safe and camouflaged.

When the state of affairs requires it, sexual slavery is constantly looming on the horizon. There are many single females who live alone, but there are plenty of women who have never been alone. Women tend to be surrounded by spouses and children.

There are all sorts of reasons why a woman might be alone: she may be divorced or widowed; she may not have children. Whatever the case, family preparedness does not always apply to women living alone.

It's no secret that in a post-SHFT situation, most women will be at a disadvantage compared to men. Men are perceived as stronger and more prone to violence. There will be quite a few things that a woman will have to deal with that men won't.

The menstrual cycle will be a challenge for getting hygiene products.

Birth control will also be a challenge.

Protecting themselves physically against surviving men and gangs.

Dealing with childbirth is not going to be easy. Childbirth would definitely be a challenge, as would take care of the kids during survival times.

Breastfeeding is the appropriate way to feed your toddler in an emergency. No preparation or sterilization is required. It is especially important to make sure your hands and nipples are clean.

If you have no milk or any formula for your infant, you might give your infant pure water; it doesn't provide nutrients but at least will stave off that hunger feeling for a short time.

Caution: Never give water to an infant under six months old; water can cause hyponatremia in infants and water intoxication.

Also, you should never put a face mask on a baby. An infant's lungs aren't always up to the task of breathing harder through them.

The woman living alone has to take extra precautions and be more vigilant at home. She must learn to use a firearm. Also, she should learn how to use some tools to be able to repair things after the SHTF.

Don't make it apparent that your house belongs to a woman alone. Be prepared to hunker down if a disaster occurs; one of the most dangerous things you can do is set out on foot.

Avoid attracting attention to your house, no matter how well-prepared you are or how tough you think you are. Plan to fortify your home in advance if something happens in complete chaos.

Woman and guns

The idea that a woman can only use certain guns because of her gender is disrespectful. Regardless of gender, if you are small-boned, not very tall, and light-weighted, you may have a problem with the recoil from large-caliber guns. If the firearm is a bad fit is going to gives you some problem using it. An average sized for beginners, is a handgun with a 5" barrel, is much easier to handle.

Avoid getting pregnant.

If you don't have a family, an AHTF situation may not be the best time to start.

Consider your options:

Condoms are one of the best methods; they are about 98% effective.

Birth control pills are a short-term solution; in a long-term survival scenario, you will run out of them.

Diaphragms are reusable and about 85% effective, making them less effective than condoms.

The Natural Rhythm method requires some record-keeping on the female part; unwanted pregnancies may still occur due to inaccurate records.

With the calendar rhythm method, you estimate the time of your ovulation. Is only about 80% effective. It is considered outdated and ineffective. This is one of the least effective techniques of birth control.

Abstinence it's 100% effective with no complications.

Withdrawal method: one way to avoid pregnancy is not to give sperm a chance to meet an egg. This technique is likewise referred to as pulling out.

For menstrual cycle days if you are out in the wilderness with no modern options, you can use clumps of grass, moss, or hay, or you can use some old cloth and stuff it.

Moon cups\ these are silicone cups to collect blood flow. These are reusable or can be washed with soap and water.

Cotton pads: thin and made out of 100% cotton, you can wash them with soap and water in an off-gird scenario.

During the course of an emergency SHTF scenario, you may want to take steps to avoid pregnancy, even if you would welcome it in another situation.

Also keep in mind that there will probably be no one to perform any major procedures if you have any complications. Maybe there is someone in your group who has or could serve as a midwife or has some medical experience to help you.

Yeast infections

Women and men can get yeast infections, which can be transmitted back and forth. Stress and hygiene can create conditions for yeast infections.

Rape is also a weapon against men because the thugs have an idea if it hurts the morale of men if the women on their side are violated. Rape could happen to men too. Many men will probably never come forward out of fear and shame.

Eliminate trading sex for survival. This idea repulses most of us. The fact is that in a desperate SFHT situation, people will find themselves doing things they never dreamed they could even think about. Don't do it; you will regret it.

Sex

STDs will increase dramatically during a SHTH scenario. During a long emergency, safe sex is not practiced much. Part of this is due to a lack of access to supplies like condoms.

Due to a lack of enforcement and consequences, people will do what they were afraid to do before. Sex trafficking is a major problem in the world, including the USA. Imagine how bad it will get in a long emergency with no police or law enforcement.

Lack of good hygiene practices can make it easier for sexual infections.

Prostitution

This is an unpopular topic that needs to be addressed.

Prostitution will become rampant. Like it or not, intercourse is a historic bartering tool. It's one that has been around since the very beginning of civilization. It is one of the oldest professions ever.

Lesson 5

Scouting

Scouting and patrolling are the skills to get out to the area surrounding your home or base camp and find out what is happening and if there is any imminent danger close by, while remaining undetected in a situation without any rule of law.

The objectives of scouting are to observe terrain and find a path through unsafe territory. Also to seek out needs like food, fuel, medical supplies, and building supplies.

Moving across an urban area in an SHTF situation is going to be a dangerous and problematic task.

You have to establish rules; someone has to be in charge; there is safety in numbers; and you have to give every person in the group a list of commands so in the field there is no dispute in order to follow.

It is very important to learn basic hand signals. You want your team to be able to communicate and move quickly and quietly without talking or yelling at each other. It is important to signal your team if you see someone before they see them.

Scouting parties are typically small, two- or three-man scouting teams; they act as the eyes and ears, gathering information for the team or group.

You should never be seen by the adversary or engage the antagonist in direct confrontation.

Conducting some scouting with your group will help you become familiar with the territory. Knowing your surroundings is essential for each survival situation.

The primary thing is to look out for signs of gangs, loot, and activities that can hurt your home or team. Also, to find out where and when it's taking bartering supplies exchanges.

Avoid roads; if you use roads, walk parallel to the road far enough away to avoid ambushes. Do the same with railroad tracks or waterways. Never camp near landmarks or open fields.

Determine danger areas; keep an eye out for areas where you can be attacked, like a hilltop or a very dark grassy area alone. Verify the route and alternative routes you and your party will be able to use and how many people you need to take with you on this particular mission.

You can expect to encounter groups. If martial law is in effect, those rough groups will be looking to loot and steal; engaging any other group is not wise.

When possible, take someone with you to operate like a team, looking out for each other and maintaining visual contact. It is important to your group's security to alter patterns by altering days to go out, times, and routes to and from.

Moving as a squat

It doesn't matter if your group is walking or biking; you must organize it in a patrol formation.

Travel in a straight line to conceal the number of people on bikes or walking. Trying to hide in the path of the person in front of you. When traveling in a line, you have a point man, approximately 20 to 30 feet ahead of the group.

Always maintaining the visibility of the patrol member in front. If the front men stop, everyone stops as well; there are no necessary orders or yelling; it is instantaneous.

If there is a threat—gangs or thugs ahead of the point line men—they only see the point man instead of the whole group. This way, the rest of the group can get ready to combat the situation from a better position; the adversary doesn't know about them.

If the unit is crowded together, everybody will most likely be wounded by incoming fire.

On a wide road, it is better to travel in a staggered line on the sides of the road, about 25 feet from the person in front of you on the opposite side of the road. Always keep the men in front visible. This allowed the groups to have an advantage.

Travel in groups if you can. You should take in your backpack a small first aid kit in case someone or yourself gets shot to stop the bleeding and the infection, a local area map, even if it is done by you, and a flash light.

Some warm jackets if it's cold, a hat, and socks in case they get wet; of course, bullets and your guns; also, a knife; and some fish net line in case you or your team need to tie or make a trap.

To avoid gangs and thugs, it is better to travel at night, but if the conflict is with the military, night operations are out; they will use night vision and thermal vision to spot people moving on the ground. If the military is involved, then travel during the day.

There are different types of night vision- Night vision gives you the capability to see in low light condition, night vision does not work in total darkness, it intensify the light existing in the region, so if there is totally dark, your night vision won't work.

Infrared gadget produce infrared light to illuminate the area, this device does not depend on ambient light.

Thermal gear do not need light, it determine the heat of the objet being watched, without any light that can be detected.

Keep in mind that during the daytime, you will be detected from a considerable distance, and you and your team can become targets very quickly.

If you must fire a firearm, most likely it will give away your location; you've got to move out right away, as quickly as possible.

In an urban scenario, it's better to look like a threat than a target. If confrontation is imminent and your group is more than three or four, your group should be walking 10 or 15 feet apart, not in a straight line, one on the left side of the sidewalk, the other on the right side.

If one person is attacked, the others can come to their aid; this way, it is harder to hurt more than one person at the same time. The one in the lead could have his weapon pointed ahead; another must point the gun to his left side; the other must point the gun to his right side; and the one in the rear must point the gun to the rear.

Avoiding tips:

Do not enter any park or inhospitable surroundings if they are particularly crowded.

Avoid foliage; hedges and tall grass or brushes can cover potential muggers.

Avoid schools at all costs. Also, stay away from hospitals; they are as dangerous as schools. You will probably find people there who stormed hospitals and schools to steal food, drugs, and a place to live. These places have big rooms, space, a kitchen, and restrooms. Depending on the situation, hospitals can also be places where you can catch some very bad infections.

Churches could give you shelter from a blizzard-like situation. It is a very dangerous place to be if there is civil unrest and mob violence going on or expected soon. It is a very dangerous place to be if there is civil unrest and mob violence going on or expected soon.

Anytime you are forced to travel, whether day or night, avoid major roads. Roads are where you find ambushes and, in many cases, traps designed to capture you.

Avoid tunnels, structures like sheds and old abandoned buildings; enter only in an emergency situation or if you have to hide and stay overnight on your excursion.

Be cautious of anyone that approaches you, or if they're walking at a distance from you, be suspicious of groups walking by.

Primary skills for Scouts

Land navigation

Range and time estimation

Camouflage

Route selection

Get out and back safely and undetected.

Leave no sign of you having passed by.

If it looks good, it's probably a trap.

Different routes out and back home

Make sure nobody is following your team back home.

Gunfire is only allowed in an emergency; gunfire can attract more people.

People are going to look for or exchange coffee, alcohol, soap, matches, blankets, flashlights, food and water, batteries, shampoo, and more. It is essential to know how to close the deal with people during a crisis.

Remember, people are willing to do anything to survive or defend their loved ones.

It is not recommended, but if the only person that can go out with you is a woman, she has to take extra precautions: her hair has to be cut short; she has to wear a tight bra to flatten her bust; she has to wear a hat and glove if it is cold; her nails have to be trim and short; she has to wear sun glasses; and she has to wear a very wide long-sleeve shirt and oversized pants to hide her curvy body.

No smells or perfumes don't show much skin; the sexier you look, the more attention and problems there will be.

I know some women who can fight and shoot and are tough and powerful. But you don't want a gang to discover her cover, and you fight with a mob trying to kidnap her to use her as a sex slave, trade her, or sell her to a gang.

Missions

Operating Procedures:

Move at night; it is much better.
Team size (two to three people per team)
Communications
Equipment
Security procedures
Always maintain security

Avoid the following:

Roads
Bridges
Civilian and military personnel

The problem is that if your group is operating in darkness and the thugs have night vision equipment, they are observing what your team is doing. They will have a clear advantage over you.

In night travel, you cannot see hazards if you are not walking on an abandoned highway to avoid detention. There are going to be tree roots and holes in the ground, which are all potential hazards you cannot see at night.

You can hurt yourself with an ankle sprain or fracture, interrupting your team's mission. Making it critical to return to base without making noises or carrying someone hurt.

If you have to cover:

Do not occupy a concealed site for more than a day. In most situations, camouflage during the day and move at night. Do not create fires or prepare food. Smoke and food smells will reveal your site. Find a place where you can rest and recuperate.

Upper floors

It is not a good idea to take shelter on upper floors; they are always the weakest and also the hardest to escape from on your own.

Evasion

When you can't escape, you've got to fight. Learn to evade threats and when to hide, run, or fight.

Scouts Assets:

Maps

Maps are very important and useful in scouting planning

Binoculars

Binoculars are one of the most important tools when you are hunkered down at home or scouting the surrounding areas. They should be small and lightweight so you can store them in your backpack, while a larger pair will certainly offer better optical performance; a small one is more practical in a SHTF situation. A pair of binoculars will be priceless.

4-way Sillcock key: This key allows you to turn on the water from the outdoor spigot of a residential or commercial building.

This is an essential tool when you are on the run and need water if there is still water in the city

Crowbar-Pry Bar: A pry bar has an angled, flattened end that allows it to be used as a lever. Crowbars are created with a curved end and an angled end that allow proper leverage. Pry bars are usually made of steel.

The crowbar or pry bar tool allows you to gain access to different buildings in case your team needs shelter. Also, you may use it as a defensive tool and to escape in an emergency by chopping through walls.

First Aid Kit: You never know when someone in your group is going to need it. Prescription medicine can be carried in a zip-lock bag, not in a bottle; bottles make noise.

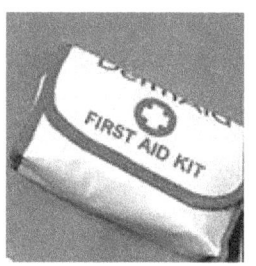

Gloves-in case you need to protect your hands or if it's cold.

Duct tape

Duct tape can be used to seal boxes, food supplies and can also be used as handcuffs if needed.

Permanent market—in case you need to leave messages for someone in your group. So it won't be erased. Use codes so only your group knows them and strangers won't understand the message.

Warm clothes-It may get cold at night, better lightweight warm clothes.

Lock Picking-Knowing how to pick locks can save your life and your team-group live.

Dogs-Be careful with dogs especially when walking across unfamiliar neighborhoods, not only because dogs may attack you, but also because of the barking can blow your cover.

If a dog attacks you, hitting with your arms or kick with your leg's, never run away because it will trigger dogs instinct to chase the prey.

Red light-If you have to use a light at night, always use a red light. Standard white light goes a long distant and will draw attention to you.

Walkie-talkie

Walkie-talkie or two ways radios are an optimal communication option in a SHTF crisis. Keep transmission short to avoid direction finding. Their greatest drawback is they use rechargeable batteries and they will useless if the battery is down.

No cameo, or commando fashions, or martial art shirt.

Tattoos may inadvertently indicate status, or affiliations, easy to remember later on. Cover them up.

Window punch-it's quitter than a rock-can be very dangerous, be extremely careful and wear gloves and long sleeve if you have to use one.

Road maps-with the route planning to navigate, but never with the way going back, in case the map get in the wrong hand, so the attackers won't know how and when the team is going to go back.

Iodine drops- is used to decontaminate water for drinking

Water portable filter-in case you need to obtain water in an emergency.

Protective Cloth

It is crucial to wear cloth to protect you from the elements, body armor if possible under a shirt, a cap, and sun glasses to protect you from glare from the sun.

Eyeglasses

Can reflect light at night and give up your location; use black tape or any color tape to conceal any shinny parts on eyeglasses or watches.

Signaling

A Polish canteen cup or a belt buckle can be used if you don't have a mirror.

Whistles

An excellent way for close signaling.

Condom

The condom also makes excellent fire tinder. The use of a latex condom will help you ignite and will burn for several minutes, allowing you sufficient time to build your fire. They make incredible small water ampules that can hold as much as 2 liters of water if handled properly.

They are designed to be watertight; the elasticity of latex condoms is shocking.

Navigation techniques

Use the location of the sun to find north.

Look at the stars at night to verify directions.

Use points of reference such as buildings, towers, and rivers to plot a route.

Prevent tracking when going back to home or compound.

Be constantly on the alert. Try to memorize every terrain feature, movement, action, and person to bring back information to your compound.

Such observation will enable you and your team on future excursions to avoid booby traps or being captured.

Good river crossing locations include:

A shallow bank or sandbar.

Cross the river downstream so that you will cross the current at about a 45-degree angle.

Tie your equipment-guns and supplies-to the top of your rucksack or in a bundle if you have no pack.

Avoid, if possible:

A deep or rapid waterfall or a deep channel

Rocky places

Don't swim or cross a stream or river when the water is very cold. This swim could be fatal.

What to do if your feet are wet

Take off your shoes; place a plastic bag on every foot; place your feet's backs in your shoes. The plastic will seize the warmth your body generates. Of course, your feet will still be wet, but they will sweat in the plastic and get warm.

You might not be able to head home; maybe your team needs to take shelter. Before getting into a building or any location, you need to be sure it is safe, accessible, and has a getaway out.

You must walk and look tough and crazy; anyone who has walked through gang territory knows this.

However, at the same time, try to keep cool and not look for trouble.

Most of the people you will encounter on the road or off it are eager to jump you, knock you down, or shoot you on sight.

You are carrying supplies they need and want; it's survival of the fittest.

Here are some Skills to survive SHFT

Shelter-how to locate and find a good location to survive, for a night or longer.

Water- you must know how and where to find water and collect it.

Time-you must know or learn to track time by the sun, it will help you immensely, when to set up your camp? Or when to move.

Fire making-a fire will help you keep warm; purify water, send signal and cook.

Orientation-you must know how to travel, where you are going or how to return, you must learn how to read a map.

Weather signs- this is a most, if a storm is reaching you, so you can prepare to hide, or move out on time.

First aid-extremely important for you or your squat team to have knowledge how to use the first aid kit.

Human waste- you must know how and where to dispose human waste.

Wild animal food- is a most that you or someone in your group knows or learns how to clean fish and get your game animal clean and ready to cook.

Knot tying- I have seen many people that didn't knew how to tie a strong knot; you must learn to do it, it is a most in a survival situation, including to tie a prisoner hands.

Swimming- Learn in a survival situation you must know how, in case you have to escape, or hide in a river or lake.

Bicycle-Most people knows how to ride a bike, if you don't know, you better learn, because in a SHTF catastrophe, when there is no fuel, a bicycle can help you move faster and obtain greater distance than walking.

Communication-you will have to come out with a way to communicate with your group, or base. Probably you won't be able to use a walkie-talkie.

Signals-learn to use a mirror and innovations your group can come out with.

Morse code-you better learn how to use it, if you don't know now. Extremely important in a SHTF.

Family defense-gangs and thugs are going to be all over the streets looking for people to assault. You must be arm and ready to protect yourself and your family.

How to cook-so people don't see the smoke or smell the food blocks away from your home base.

Food rationing-Somebody has to be in control of rationing food and water.

Weapons in top notch- Maintaining your weapons working clean and ready is a job you can't take lightly.

Livestock-Keeping your livestock healthy, hidden, and protective is a must.

Cloth-Somebody has to be in charge of washing the cloths and sewing them.

Gardening- someone has to take care of the survival garden and the growing food.

Tutoring and teaching the kids-tough job-difficult after SHTF

In command- a person must be in charge if there is a group, so there are not back and forth when an order is giving.

Lessen 6

Ambushes

They strike when you least expect them. Example: A hidden clothesline will knock you off your bike or motorcycle, or a sniper will target you and shout at you as you drive by.

They will make the roads nearest their home heavily fortified. To keep their home safe, they don't want outsider driving or walking by.

When walking on dirt roads, stay in the middle of the road, go slow and keep your eyes open, and ears alert.

The important of being conscientious about sound is critical. You must remain quiet always and particular in movements. Your team must have disciplined about this.

It is a good idea for your party to take along knifes or a smaller.22 in in case you have to use it, it will generate a lot less sound than a big caliber rifle or gun.

Boots are a better choice for certain terrains; boots give you better traction and better ankle support. If you can get a hold of tactical boots, they are great, they are designed to be fast and light weight, and excellent to walk in a not known terrain.

Just make sure you can walk easily and run comfortably should you need to, no matter what you wear.

If anyone in you groups forced to defend himself, avoid firing a firearm if you can, use bows, slingshot, knives anything that won't draw attention. If you fire a gun, after the conflict it's over get the hell out as fast you can.

To survive in a street confrontation you have to learn how to think like a Predator. You have to be able to foresee who is likely to ambush you, attack, try to rape you or robbed you.

As your team increases the range, it will take more time to get back home; you will be exposed for longer periods of time.

Estimate the time you need to scavenge a site and never rush. You don't want to make a mistake, noise or injure yourself.

Emergency shelters can be constructed with tarps, natural materials. debris and by taping two or three big trash bags together.

Sleeping location

If your team or you need to sleep and recuperate for a few hours, the first thing to do is find protection from the weather. You are vulnerable to attacks as you sleep. Select a site to sleep, shielded from view.

Wherever you decide to sleep, make sure you can spot anyone approaching before they get too close. If you are with your 2-3-man team, take turns sleeping while one is on the lookout.

If people find your camp, you need to have at least one, or better yet, two escape routes that you can use to slip away unnoticed.

Noise, light—finding a concealed location to rest is one of the important issues, but it is also very important to keep quiet in the dark with no light.

Leave no evidence that your team slept in that location after you left, so no one can suspect anything and begin to be curious about where you came from and where you are going next.

Be extra careful with abandoned buildings you could take as a former short refuge; many other people could also be there or be planning to get there soon.

Rooftops

Be careful entering and exiting buildings; be sharp-eyed about exit points; check and find out emergency escape routes to avoid dead-end situations.

If you can access a rooftop, it could give you a decent amount of safety and security for a short time; probably your camp will be invisible to those walking by, and the downside is that rooftops usually do not provide a lot of escape options.

Something else to keep in mind is that there will be taller buildings around you, which provides a good point to see you and your team.

If you camp for the night, fires can alert people from miles away to your location, and ashes from a campfire on the ground can tell trackers how long it has been since you were there. They could also follow you back to your home, putting your family in danger.

Avoid camps with fire. You may have to navigate at night, avoid groups, keep your eyes open, walk fast but without making noises, or even try not to talk between your group members. If you are moving through the night, you cannot shine flashlights or wave lit lanterns if you want to stay concealed.

A blackout condition must be enforced in your group to avoid detention. Be careful if somebody in your group smokes; the smell can also give your crew away.

Sleep in abandoned buildings, riverbanks, underpasses, or rooftops of abandoned buildings. Always making sure there is another way out to get away.

It is possible that you'll have to walk for extra miles, even days, to return home because of obstacles in the way back home to avoid gangs and throngs.

Don't penetrate a barrier if it can be avoided or circumnavigated. Climb rooftops to obtain a better view of the area; be careful; it may be hard to climb back down.

Improvising to assist your group when climbing: two-by-fours, pipes, dumpsters, boxes, rope, belts, and cloth are items that may come in handy.

Be extra careful when going down or up the stairs when entering a building. Avoid junk cars or bad-shaped streets and sidewalks.

Establish escape routes.

Make sure to locate multiple escape routes for each dwelling you visit, rest in, or stay in overnight. Keep in mind that glass breaks, and drywall is breakable. Exit doesn't mean doors are necessary.

Self-defense

Knowledge, awareness, proper behavior and the ability to recognize the dangerous situation on the spot, fast without thinking, just like a reflex or like you breathe.

Maybe you have a close personal encounter and you have to fight. You can subdue your attacker, and the best response is:

Eye gouging: It sounds simple, but stabbing the eyes should be the first move done in a close-up self-defense situation. You can really hurt them.

Strike using the palm of your hand in an upward motion against their nose. The nose is extremely sensitive and a hard strike like this can break it or make bleed.

Ear slapping or tearing: slap and try to tear the ear off.

By hitting the throat or the windpipe, if you strike with enough force, you can kill the aggressor. This move should be used with that in mind and only in a life-or-death situation.

Groin: If you are at close range, bring your knee up, snap, and bring it back. Repeat a second later to make sure you strike his groin. It is a great move. The emphasis here is on speed.

Younger Author

Biting: This technique is brutal; you could bite the aggressor if he is grappling you at close range to each other. You could bite his neck, chest, arms, and legs. This is also dangerous to you; the attacker may be sick or infected, and you may get his disease. Everything is on the line when it comes to your own survival. It's either you or them, so you can't have mercy or restraint. You must act.

Head-butt-backward: if the attacker is grabbing you from behind, jerk your head back as hard as you can and hit him with a head-butt in the face. The same can be done with a front head-butt strike if he is grabbing you close from the front.

Cathole

Cathole is used to dispose bowel movements or waste water from camping. A Cathole should be dug 6-8 inches deep and at least 150 feet from water, trails and campsites.

For number 2, if you are on the move, your best option is to dig a Cathole. Just dig a hole to relive yourself. Once you are done, fill the hole with the dirt you dug up and cover the spot with leaves.

Snow walking

When walking in snow, don't take shortcuts in areas where snow and ice removal is not possible. Walk slowly, take short steps, or shuffle for balance. It is very dangerous if all of a sudden you are faced with adversaries.

Basic instruction

Whenever you are using a knife, hatchet, or anything with a blade, cut away from yourself.

Set up your shelter during daytime hours; don't wait until 6 p.m. or 7 p.m. waiting until the sun goes down can be dangerous because injuries can easily happen.

How to treat gunshot wounds

The first thing is, like, the most important—check if the victim is still alive and is still breathing. If the answer is yes, then find out if their airway passage is clean. Keep the airway open and clear if the victim is still breathing; if not, begin CPR. I assume that you or someone in your group knows how to do it.

Controlling the bleeding could be the difference between life and death.
Clean the wound.
Close the wound with sutures, glue, etc.
Wrap any garb around the injury.
Conscious victims sit or lie in a position that is comfortable for them.
Unconscious victims should be placed in the recovery position.
Don't give the wounded anything to eat or drink.
There could be internal bleeding, which you can do nothing about.

Do not elevate the legs if the gunshot wound is above the waist, unless the gunshot is in the arm. Wounds to the abdomen and chest will bleed more quickly if the legs are elevated, making it harder for the victim to breathe.

Anything you use to get the bullet out should be sterilized and cleaned of any dirt. Alcohol will be okay. The wound must be cleaned, disinfected, and sewn back at home.

If the bullet remains in the body, an infection may progress and make the condition worse.

It is possible the gunshot will be lethal for the victim.

Communication is important when potential threat is spotted. If using a radio or walkie talkies use a fake name. The truth is that if you or anybody in your group get shoot at, your guys will shoot back and usually doesn't end well for at least one of the group. Also shooting will alert other potential assailant of your position.

Scouting survival actions:

Learn to jump start a car you may need to do it at any time.

Gas Siphoning**:**

There could be a time when you will need how to properly siphon gas in a safety way in a hurry; this could save your life and the lives of your team. This is the old-fashioned way of getting the glow of gas started by sucking through the hose with your mouth in an emergency.

In a SHTF situation, your scouting squad will probably be walking or biking, depending on the magnitude of the situation. If the need or opportunity arises, you may need to siphon gas for any vehicles you may have, such as motorcycles, motorbikes, pick-up trucks, or maybe a generator.

You must understand that there is danger in siphoning gas this way. Gasoline and diesel are dangerous materials; both are very toxic and can give you serious problems if you inhale their fumes or ingest them by accident. Not only are you drinking a bit, but the fumes are very dangerous with the suction method.

Also remember that before you begin siphoning, you should never light a cigarette, and make sure there is no flame or someone smoking close by.

How to siphon gasoline with your mouth:

You only need a single hose and a container close by.

Feed one end of the hose into the gas tank until it is entirely submerged near the bottom.

The next step is to suck the end of the hose to get the gasoline out of the tank.

Suck on the hose only with your mouth to create pressure.

As soon as the flow of gas is rising near your lips, crinkle the hose to stop the flow of gas. If you don't do this in time, you will get some gasoline in your mouth.

Drop the hose into your gas container, and gravity will do the rest of the work, letting gas flow freely from the tank to your container.

If you get some gas in your mouth, spit it out right away.

To start again, you will need to drain the hose before starting again.

Problem with siphon and new vehicles:

The new vehicles have a safety anti-siphoning mechanism between the nozzle and the gas tank to prevent stealing fuel; the old vehicles don't have it. You can go around this by easily holding the barrier with a screwdriver.

You will pry open the little flaps while you are sucking the gasoline out. Remember, it has a very dangerous smell, and swallowing a little bit of gas is dangerous.

Bicycle or bike stock in mud:

If your bicycle or motorcycle is stuck in mud, drag the stuck wheel sideways out of the rut. Then, when you reach the ground, pick up the bike like you always do in any drop.

Patch a bike tire:

In an emergency, cut a three-inch piece of electrical tape or duct tape. Position the piece of tape over the hole, making sure it is in the center of the strip. Wrap the tape totally around the tube.

Another way to use it in an emergency is to stuff the tire full of leaves. You could also use newspapers to load the tire.

How to jumpstart a motorcycle without a battery

Turn the key to the on position; make sure the kill switch is in the on position.

Stand on the left side of the bike and grasp both handlebar grips.

Set the bike in 2nd or 3rd gear.

With the bike in gear, grasp the clutch and get the bike rolling; once rolling, release the clutch.

Rev-push forward until it starts

One of the most important recovery tactics for vehicles is:

Star a car-pickup truck

This technique only works with cars and pickup trucks that have manual transmissions.

Position the ignition to on.

Set the gearbox to the second shift.

Press down on the clutch pedal.

The individual or group outside the car or truck starts pushing the vehicle.

Wait for the car or truck to gain some speed, then gradually release the clutch and slowly press the gas pedal.

This method of push-starting is the most reliable way to start a car or pickup truck; it should start after the last step. If it doesn't, repeat the steps again.

How to get a pickup truck out of the mud:

Put your vehicle in park.

Grab your car mat out and position the tip of the mat under the stuck tire, with the rest of the mat in front of the tire.

Get back into the car and drive slowly forward until you reach solid ground.

Rock back and forward action

You can also try the rock back and forward action to get your pickup truck stuck out. Maintain the wheels straight, softly press down the gas pedal, and rock the car forward and back by switching between drive and reverse. Slowly drive out.

Pull your pickup truck out of the mud.

An additional way to do it is to dig the dirt or snow away from your tire; this is an extremely useful tool for getting a vehicle unstuck. You can use your hands, a shovel, a rock—anything can be used.

Avoid Wheel spin

Flooring the gas is a massive mistake; it creates a wheel spin and only worsens the trouble. If you are driving a manual, drive in second or third gear to keep a steady pace.

Deflates your tire action:

Another way to try to get your vehicle out of the mud is to deflate your tires to increase their contact patch.

Rope tip:

Rope: Have a rope just in case you get stuck in a ditch. If you tie your car to a tree, by pulling the rope at a perpendicular angle halfway between the car or truck and the tree, you can exert enough leverage to pull your car or open-bed truck out of a ditch.

A rope is very useful and handy to have, especially in a survival situation. Ropes and their use dates back for many years, you can use them for hunting, pulling, attaching, transporting, lifting and climbing.

There are different kinds of ropes:

| Light duty rope | Medium duty rope | Heavy duty rope |

Here are a few samples:

Paracord: is well known and popular to carry for outdoor activities. People also call it "550 Paracord because it has a breaking load of 550 lbs. (249 kg).

Kevlar rope: synthetic rope it is a very strong rope, so strong that many people use it to replace steel cables in construction.

Polypropylene rope: this rope is water-resistant, floats in the water. Excellent choice; it will resist mildew.

Wire rope: strands of metal wire rotated into a helix composite rope, used to lift, position, attach, remove, and brace.

Manila is very popular in landscape use, but it shrinks when it gets wet. Keep this consideration in mind.

Twine rope is an excellent selection for pulleys, blocks, and is resistant to abrasion and chemicals.

Bank line rope is often used by fishermen to make trotlines for fishing; this is where it gets its name. Most of the time, it is black.

Ropes tensile strength and working load are characteristics you must learn about. Tensile strength indicates the maximum load a rope can support before it breaks.

The working load is the range of weight that is safe to use before it snaps.

Crowbar:

The practical thing about a crowbar is that it has several uses in an emergency; one of them is self-defense. Crowbars are excellent tools for opening doors.

How to use it to open doors:

Introduce the crowbar into the gap between the door frame and the lock, where it will push the lock out toward you. Put on force with the crowbar, pushing away from you. This will generate a strong pressure on the lock, which should snap or break the lock out of its position, allowing you to get inside. The wider the slit between door and frame, the easier it is to open.

If the deadbolt lock has a short bolt, it will allow the door to be opened with a crowbar.

Destructive devices

Destructive devices include explosives, incendiary bombs, grenades, Molotov cocktails, or glass bottles filled with gasoline that ignites their fuse when broken. Destructive devices are illegal to possess under federal law, as are similar devices.

I'm giving you information on how to make one for educational purposes only. They are very dangerous; you can get your face and arms burned. The information given here is only educational; for the end of the world, it may become useful to know how it is made.

The author and publisher are not responsible for any damage, present or future, you may obtain because of this educational disclosure. Remember, it is against federal law to make and use explosives like this, and we don't recommend making one.

A Molotov cocktail is not a basic bomb, usually consisting of a bottle filled with flammable liquid and a wick that is ignited before being thrown. A Molotov cocktail is not an explosive device; it is intended to start a fire, and it usually doesn't explode in the hand of the guy throwing it.

How to make a Molotov

Fill the bottle with the mixture, of flammable substances gasoline, kerosene, etc., around 34 ounces or less if there is a small amount of liquid.

Introduce one half of the wick into the bottle so that it is filled with liquid.

Insert half of the wick tightly into the neck of the bottle so that the liquid won't leak out.

Molotov Cocktail
F.M

Wrap the neck of the bottle with a rag and fix it with a slice of Scotch tape so you don't get burned while throwing it.

The end of the wick coming out should not be long; 4 or 5 cm will be enough.

Just wet it just before throwing the cocktail

Light the wick and throw it at the objective.

Safety:

It must not be open flames close to a ready bottle; it is going to be very flammable. Make your cocktail outdoors in a well-ventilated area. Acetone and gasoline fumes can be harmful to your health.

Leave the end wick dry until ready to throw.

<u>Remember, it is against federal law to make explosive-flammable devices.</u>

He will win who knows when to fight and when to not to fight
Sun Tzu

Lesson 7

Bartering

Bartering is a dangerous situation during a collapse; you can be scammed, hurt, or killed. You don't know if the other party will meet their end of the deal.

Cash at the beginning of the first few days after the SHTF will be a lifesaver, whether to buy essential food or even relocate your family. Sooner or later, surviving with money becomes useless; without a government to ensure the currency, people will return to the barter system. The current money will be considered worthless.

You may have to break into grocery stores, pharmacies, or warehouses, probably breaking doors to get supplies or smashing windows. Smashing windows will draw attention; it is far better to pick a way in without making noises.

Do not openly brandish firearms unless your life is in danger and you must defend yourself.

People will be looking for coffee, alcohol, matches, blankets, shampoo, soap, food, water, etc. You have to find a way to exchange items and make deals with them.

Gold

It is a fact that valuable metals maintain their value even in a crisis. Gold is a great investment, as it will retain its high value even after a very long economic collapse.

Best bartering items:

Antibiotics: Everybody will be looking for them in an apocalypse, as they will fight against bacterial infection, which could lead to more bacteria or, at worst, death.

Eggs and chicken are both invaluable bartering items.

Seeds: Beans are easy to grow and preserve. Spinach is cold-hardy and prolific; carrots require little space.

Squash and pumpkin are prolific producers. Allium varieties include onions, shallots, and garlic, and beets are easy to grow and multifunctional.

Bandages: people will also be looking for bandages for their ability to protect wounds from infections.

Painkillers: basic painkillers such as ibuprofen, Tylenol, and aspirin will be at the top of the list.

Knives and saws: These items can be used for various purposes, like woodworking, cooking, hunting, or protection.

Flashlights, matches, lighters, and candles: these items will help people through the night when there is no electricity. Likewise, they can be used to create fire to cook.

Liquor or coffee: are not required for survival, but people will do anything to obtain them.

Tobacco: isn't required for survival, but for people addicted to it, it will be hard to say no to these items.

Clothing, blankets, and shoes: shelter, warmth, and comfort—are necessary to protect oneself from the elements.

Toothpaste and brushes: During an economic collapse, dental health is important, but a dentist will be almost impossible to find.

Hygiene items: toilet paper, women's Kotex, pads, and other period supplies—are going to be at the top of the list when it comes time to barter.

Tools of all kinds will be excellent for bartering. People will need to rebuild.

Condoms: Nobody will want a pregnancy or a baby in the middle of a disaster.

Salt, sugar, and spices: these ingredients will be luxury items.

Skills: construction, plumbing, nursing, carpentry. Caution: do not bring any strangers home (more on this in the final thought page at the end of the book).

Duct tape: Duct tape is versatile and can be used for many occasions; it is likely to have great value for bartering.

Handcarts and wheel barrows: these items will make work lighter. To use them for gardening, feeding animals, or doing other labor that requires moving heavy materials.

Plastic bags: have many uses, like sanitary disposal and much more.

Fuel is very hard to find.

Fishing and hunting supplies: These supplies allow people to procure their own food and will be of great value.

Weapons and ammo: These are items you want and need to keep for yourself. You don't want somebody using your bullets against you later on.

Woman hygiene products.

The important key to surviving is knowing how to scavenge for the things you need. One of the most satisfactory things to get is an automobile battery or an alternator. Use them to make an easy windmill or a watermill to boost the battery.

Barter in different locations each time if it is possible. This will keep looters and bandits from calculating your schedule, the days you are showing up, and your time.

Keep a low profile; you don't want guys to suspect you're hiding more than you are showing. Act accordingly.

It is not recommended that you go out with a woman; she has to take extra precautions, like I said before in another part of this book.

She most often wears an extra-wide long-sleeve shirt and oversized pants to hide her curvy body. Don't show much skin; the more attention she brings, the more problems there will be.

Scavenger

Scavenging is the act of taking or gathering material from discarded or abandoned property. In contrast, looting is the act of stealing or taking goods by force, often associated with rioting.

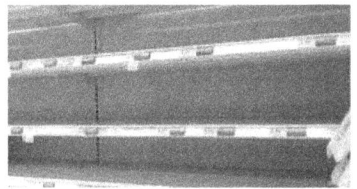

Looting is something criminals do without any reasons. Scavenging is what survivors do to ensure their survival. The grocery stores, food markets, and pharmacies will be empty because of looters.

Basic steps of scavenging

Make a list of items you need.

Prioritize those needs.

Find the area you want to scavenge; avoid populated areas; items may already be gone; you don't want the risk of being seen.

Scout the area before heading there to make sure it is safe to enter.

Collect the goods and make sure you have the means to carry them back home.

Store the goods: you need to know how and where you plan to store the goods you scavenge. Probably you will need to break into buildings and you will need something to carry your supplies, such as a large cart with rolling wheels; a grocery cart will be helpful.

You will need to take with you a crowbar or a window breaker. Also, a flashlight will be good to take along.

Be attentive; people turn quick into violence if they perceive you in their minds as looting.

You can look for supplies in places like garages, vending machines, and the school cafeteria, and keep in mind that you won't be the only one scavenging for supplies.

I will focus on smaller places rather than big places like malls, which most people will target first.

Here is a list of some places to consider:

Abandoned farms	Processing factories
Abandoned stores	Abandoned supplies truck
Ships, trains, and autos	Hospitals junkyard
Warehouses	Abandoned gyms
Abandoned schools	Store units
Junkyards	Landfills

Office building: offices will have water and a small kitchen.

Amusement parks, zoos, and cinemas will have food, water, supplies, and maintenance tools.

Pawn shops—these will have tools, gold, and silver.

Animal feed is important if you have pets.

Marinas and boat yards: sources of food and emergency equipment

Self-storage units are usually secure, so it's worth a shot.

New schools—for sure, they will have a kitchen with canned foods and equipment, as well as first aid and some clothing.

Abandoned vehicles need supplies like batteries and fuel.

The idea is to check abandoned places far away from primary streets. Considering your survival needs before you go out to get provisions:

Do you have enough food?

Do you have water?

Do you have enough medical supplies?

Communication

Non-verbal and verbal communication:

Communication will be an issue when the power grid breaks down.

It is a good idea to carry an old-school communication device such as a ham radio or CB radio. The only drawback to these devices is that they require a power supply. Cell phones won't work. Probably you won't be able to talk with relatives if they live far away.

Radios are great, but under certain circumstances, they may not work or reach you from far away.

If there has been an EMP attack that has damaged communications, it will be almost impossible to contact your family.

During an emergency, the most useful frequencies will be within the HAM radio bands. The ultimate survivalist choice is simple amateur radio and can be as simple or complex as you like. It can reach not only your area but also around the world.

GMRS: Walkie-Talkies are a good choice for emergency use. GMRS are good for long-range versatility. GMRS walkie-talkies are as affordable as FRE or MURS units, but in my opinion, they can do much more.

As of today, it does require a license to operate a ham radio. The Federal Communications Commission (FCC) has strict rules for the kind of radios that can be used that meet with the requirement.

There are three levels:

General, technician, and extra.

Repeaters allow you to signal over much larger distances; your signal can originate from any point in the world.

You would need to upgrade your antenna for longer distances; many people disguise their antennas so they are not visible to others, and people place antennas on fences, flagpoles, and ladders.

Walkie-talkies they are very simple to use and allow two-way communication over a short distance. The down side is that if anyone else is on the same channel, they will be listening to every word you say.

The CB radio could be a good option if you have somebody within a few miles of you who knows to meet on a specific channel. Having a good multiband ham radio will allow you to send and receive critical emergency information during a disaster. It is also a great way to find alternative news from around the world.

You will know accurately what is going on, and you will get much more accurate details. Unless each group has ham radios with backup electric technology systems, you won't be speaking with them. Without mail facilities, no letters may be sent.

There are a few devices with hand cranks instead of electricity; they are great because hand cranks are mini electrical generators, and maybe you can hear the radio if there is a station and get some information.

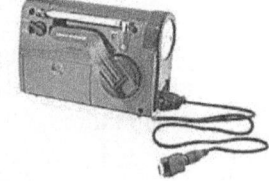

Two famous ones are radios and storm lanterns. They won't give you a lot of energy, but they will make you able to listen to the radio and get a light source without grid power.

You also need to come up with a non-verbal way to communicate with your group in case you have to try to re-enter your home or compound to let them know everything is okay and they are not forcing you to try to get inside.

Morse code

In emergency situations, code is very important. People could see you dropping your note and use the information to try to steal your supplies or find out where your home base or compound is. You can use Morse code or come up with your own system.

You can improvise and use a flag system or use a flashlight to send signals in Morse code. You could wait for your scouting team to come back in at a specific time and signal them using a code.

The use of whistle blows or horn blasts to communicate with people close by has been used for thousands of years.

If worst comes to worst and you need to communicate over very long distances, you could send a messenger as a last resort. Be careful what you write in the note; it could be intercepted, and you may need to rely on code to be safe.

Scanners, if they are still working somehow, are great for listening to local police activity in your area, along with Ham, aviation, and military activities.

Transportation

Bicycle-Motor Bike-Motorcycle-Moped-Truck-Car-Boat-Canoe-Kayak

When disaster strikes, mobility can be the difference between life and death. Knowing which vehicles are available and which will serve you best in a survival situation is essential.

You must be prepared to fight to defend your transportation.

You may be killed for your transportation. The mode of transportation you choose should be the best you can do with the resources you have.

The following is a list of essential advantages:

Good working order	Water crossing, if possible
Necessary storage	The ability to blend in
Distance capable	

Extra clothing and cold weather

The number one outdoor killer in the United States is hypothermia. In extreme conditions, you can die in as little as three hours without proper shelter. You must prepare for this.

What to do if your feet get cold and wet

Take off your shoes, position a plastic bag on each foot, and then place your feet back in your shoes. The plastic will retain the heat your body produces.

Yes, your feet will still be wet. But they'll be warm.

The bicycle

Is the easiest means of transportation because most of us knew how to ride as kids. It can fit in an apartment. The good point is that you won't call attention to yourself, especially when traveling at night. You can pass gang-occupied territory and dubious residences undetected unless you pass close to them.

A bicycle can take the rider an unlimited distance, and if you have to hide, you can bring it into an abandoned building or hire it in the bushes. On a bicycle, you can cover much more ground than by walking or running.

The bad point is that you are slow, you can't get out of a bad situation fast, and you are exposed to gangs, thieves, or a shooter. Being slow, you can be removed from your bike extremely easily, especially if you come upon a large group. If someone gets to you, they are taking the bike plus whatever you have on you.

Bicycles don't need batteries and are still way faster than walking. A person can walk about 3 miles per hour, but a bicycle can easily cover about 10 to 30 miles, depending on the road or weather. Still, you are going to need something faster.

Bicycles provide many advantages: they require no fuel, are easy to maintain, are lightweight, and are almost silent. You can easily scavenge parts or find another one. The bottom line is that bikes are reliable, easy to operate, easy to maintain, easy to hide, and they get you from point A to point B. Of course, you want a bike that is as lightweight as possible.

If you needed to walk, you could strap your heavy bag onto the bicycle and simply push it along, as opposed to having to carry the backpack on your back.

Tires need something inside, in the middle between the rubber and the rim. Air is preferable, but in an emergency, dirt, pine needles, three bars, and even old clothes can make it usable.

You could stock up or look for and find, if you are lucky, tubeless tires, airless bike tires, stuck-up puncture-resistant tires, or self-sealing tires. Last, there are liquid sealants, like Orange Seal, and another one is Stan's No Tubes; these are the two most popular brands, and you could find them at a local bike shop.

If you are smart, you could keep some of this for an emergency or, after the SHTF, search for it at an abandoned bike store. Or barter for some items you have.

Bicycles are capable of going places few other vehicles can manage, and bikes are also easily camouflaged and concealed.

Gas-powered motorized bicycle

A motorized bike in reality is a bicycle that has a motor connected to power the wheels. You can actually pedal if you run out of gas. Its full efficiency, you could get some outrageous miles per gallon in a situation when there is no gas; there is a big difference between a motorbike and a truck or other motorized vehicle. In my personal opinion, this is the best of the vehicles to use after the SHTF.

It is considered that maintenance is easy compared to other motor vehicles. Knowing the rider can still ride without pedaling in case of injury or even get out of a dangerous situation in a matter of minutes is comforting.

The average motorbike travel distance is about 100 mpg or more.

Another advantage is that a gas bicycle can get up to 35 mph and sometimes even more.

It all depends on:

Road condition: terrain, weather, rain, wind, rider style.

Like on a motorcycle, you should cover all of your lights: headlights and taillights. To navigate at night, use duct tape and leave a small area exposed in the shape of a rectangle in your headlight, just to allow some light to escape so you can navigate. So you don't give your position at night.

Just like on a motorcycle, tape all reflective parts, such as the chrome bumper, so if you travel during the daytime, the reflection will be seen very far away.

Pros will go almost anywhere.

Cons: The rider would be exposed to vulnerable attack from thrown objects, gunfire, arrows, limited carrying capacity, and exposure to the elements.

You also need basic tools to perform maintenance.

A set of screwdrivers, Alan wrenches

Repairs:

Flat tire-patching the inner tube-fixing or replacing brakes

Fixing and oiling the chain; replacing screws

Mopeds

Is not as good as a motorcycle since it can't go as fast or over rough terrain. Mopeds are fuel-efficient. You may need to go off-road for security reasons.

The small size of a moped limits the payload that can be carried.

Battery-powered mopeds are good if you have a solar system to recharge the batteries when the power grid melts down.

Motorcycle

When survival is eminent, your ability to move quickly could make a life-or-death difference. Few vehicles can compare to a motorcycle in an emergency escape.

Can carry some load, one can escape riots, protests, and dangerous situations fast. Dark colors are important; we are better off with no shining colors.

Fuel will quickly become scarce. Motorcycles and motorbikes use considerably less fuel than cars and trucks, making them a better choice to use. Motorcycles standard tanks unusually hold from 3 to 5 gallons, so you should get at least 55 MPG.

The common motorcycle can travel approximately 150–250 miles on one tank of fuel without refueling. Touring motorcycles can reach a fuel range of 300 miles.

It all depends on:

Road condition

Weather-rain-wind

Terrain Rider style

On a motorcycle, you can carry a surprising amount of stuff. You can strap all sorts onto the back and sides and carry them effortlessly. Most motorcycles suffer from a lack of storage.

Saddlebags are the obvious choice to add a large storage area.

No protection from the weather could be a major concern in some areas of the country. Snow will slow or stop you completely, as will ice.

Speed and elusiveness are the main reasons why motorcycles work well as scout vehicles. When survival is crucial and you need to move quickly, few land vehicles can compare to a motorcycle.

A motorcycle can drive on narrow trails with proper tires. Mud and even snow are not problems for a motorcycle.

Just about every basic bike has some off-road capability, making it more versatile than a car or most pickup trucks.

I have been a rider all of my life. My father bought me a Yamagishi 125 cc when I was in 7th grade; later in high school, I bought a Bear Yamaha 250 cc; later, I bought a Honda Bonneville 750 cc with cruise control; I still have it; it is an antique now. My son, who is also a rider owns many motorcycles too, and we used to ride to the Florida Keys together all the time.

I have ridden my motorcycle on train tracks, dirty roads, and even on a Florida Everglades trail, and I can assure you that when you need speed, a motorcycle can take you out fast in the blink of an eye.

Ideally, your bike should be kept in a secure garage to protect it from the elements and because it is easier to steal.

The author

Never carry extra fuel on your person. In the event of a crash or an attack, having something highly flammable strapped directly to you is a great risk.

You should disable all of your lights; if the grid goes down, I doubt it will matter. Head lights, tail lights, you will need some sort of headlight to navigate at night; use duct tape to complete tape off the lights and leave a small area exposed in the shape of a rectangle.

Like one inch tall and three inches wide to allow just enough light to escape so you can navigate. So you don't give your position at night.

Tape all reflective parts on the motorcycle, including the chrome bumper. If you travel during the daytime, the reflection will be seen very far away.

When equipped with suitable tires, the motorcycle can be capable of going over more rugged terrain than a car or even a truck.

Troubleshooting a motorcycle is simple compared to working on or fixing a 4x4 truck. When your motorcycle breaks down, you push it to a secure spot for repairs or camouflage, and you go ahead on foot.

Pros: They will go almost anywhere.

Cons: The rider would be exposed to vulnerable attack from thrown objects, gunfire, arrows, limited carrying capacity, and exposure to the elements. To use a motorcycle, you must consider

Flat-proofing your tires as much as possible so you can ride over debris or other sharp objects if you have to.

If you can, use protection like an armor plate or a good helmet.

Estimate:

Gas tank size (Gal.)	Fuel range: 50 MPG bike (miles)
2	100
3	150
4	200
5	250
6	300

Motorcycle (cc)	Average MPG	Average fuel range (miles)
50	100-150	150-200
125	90-125	150-400
250	50-90	150-300
300-500	50-80	150-300
600	30-50	150-300
700-950	30-80	150-350
1000+	30.-50	150-400

Truck and car

Items necessary and hard to get after the SHTF: you could try to find these parts on cars left on the highway because they ran out of gas or were abandoned after an attack. Anyhow, you are going to have a hard time locating any of these needed parts.

Fuel filter	Belts
Brakes	Batteries
Wiper blades	Oil
Tires	

You also need a stout tow chain if you find yourself in a difficult situation. To take a truck off the road, you need a pretty big path and sufficient clearance. A truck and a car will need more gasoline; a truck and a car are harder to hide and harder to drive.

They are going to be impossible to drive because of cars left in the streets blocking most of the main streets, plus the gangs will see you right away.

ATV

An all-terrain ATV is defined as a motorized off-highway vehicle.

Farmers and ranchers in all parts of the United States rely upon all-terrain vehicles (ATVs) to finish loads of tasks associated with farming and agriculture.

Three-wheeled ATVs are not being manufactured due to the fact that four-wheeled ATVs are tons safer. It is a great alternative; they have excellent gas mileage, are quiet, can ride over rough terrain, and the most common repair you will be doing is fixing a flat tire.

Although slower than a dirt bike or motorcycle, it may be better equipped for riding through the wasteland. You can store spare gear on the front and rear racks.

Under certain circumstances, the ATV can be a great survival vehicle; for example, you can carry firewood and water or use it as a surveillance vehicle.

The down side is noise; you can hear an ATV a few miles away. There are silencers readily available, but I doubt you could get your hands on one in an SHTF situation.

Non-engine-powered vehicles

Handcarts

Is the simplest method of transportation. A two-wheeled handcart can carry a couple hundred pounds, depending on the terrain on which you are going to use it.

Garden carts

A garden cart could be a good choice if you have small children who are too small to walk. A garden cart may be the answer to transporting them. It's not a good idea to go out and gather information.

Horses

Riding a horse can allow you to travel through wooded areas and over terrain that a car or even an ATV cannot. Horses can also be used to transport children, elderly, or injured human beings from your group.

Horses can be used for such tasks as pulling out three stumps, moving fences, etc.

The problem with horses is that they require care, food, medicine, proper foot care, and proper shelter. Most horses' food comes from forage materials. You can choose to grow your own grass from pasture and hay. Just like any other animal, horses can get sick or develop a disease.

Horses' feet and legs are their lifelines. Horses' hooves have to be trimmed on a regular basis to prevent their hooves from getting too long. If they are not trimmed, it can result in severe abnormalities in their feet and legs.

In a SHTF state of affairs, it is going to be tough to discover a farrier, so you ought to learn how to trim and shoe your horse in an emergency.

Crossing water may be worrying for a lot of horses. Unexpected or loud noises can cause a horse to bolt rear up or back away abruptly. If you plan to use a horse, make certain that is calm with nearby loud noises, including shouting and gun shots.

In a survival state of affairs, having to dismount to open or close a gate can waste time. Practice so you can open the gate and close it without dismounting.

If you use a horse-drawn carriage, you can travel between 10 and 30 miles a day. The only problem is that you have to use open trails and streets, and you will be visible.

Another problem is that you need to store food supplies, build a stable, and have a lot of land, or a mini-farm. Something that most of us don't have in a city. Also, there will be people who will try to still the horse for the meat.

Oxen

They are slower than horses, but they are stronger; they need attention, food, medicine, and shelter. Similar problem as with the horse.

Goat or sheep

Can be attached to a cart, is smaller, and needs attention and care, similar to the problem with the horses.

Boats

You will have an advantage if you live along the shores of navigable waters. The majority of the population will not have access to a boat of any kind. It is usually easier to fish and get fresh food right off your deck than to spend many hours hiking around the bushes hunting.

Unfortunately, boats are not usually big enough to be used as live-in boats after the SHFT; you need closet space to keep supplies like food, water, clothes, medicine, firearms, and bullets.

You can be vulnerable to shallow water, stumps, and gunfire, which can damage the hull to the point where it is taking on water and making it inoperable. If you use a sailboat, have a backup engine just in case you need to outrun someone chasing you.

Also, the best defense you could have in a boat is to remain hidden.

Inflatable boat

The main advantage of inflatable boats is that they are lightweight, don't take up a lot of space, and many of them accommodate four people. Be careful with the color; generally, inflatable boats are made in bright colors intended to be noticed easily, which is precisely what you don't desire post-SHTF.

Canoe

A canoe has been used by indigenous people around the world for thousands of years and is still used today in many places.

Today's canoes are light and modern. A good canoe is an easily propelled vessel that can carry a load over a variety of water conditions, from placid rivers and lakes to whitewater rapids.

They are silent; you can carry your supplies and guns and transport two or three guys, and if you camouflage them, you can travel without being detected.

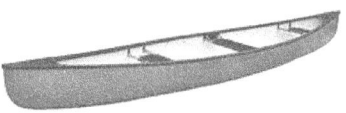

Not only does a canoe go really fast on a river, but it also helps you cross a river that would otherwise be too dangerous. They are fast, quiet, need no filling, and allow you to put more stuff inside than just your backpack.

The Shallow Arch canoes are the most popular canoes, most canoe are intended for one or two persons, some are made for more than two people.

A canoe usually has more space and a greater weight capacity than a kayak. As the city falls into chaos, the overwater route in the city can be a first-rate protection option.

With the right preparation, equipment, and mindset, the ultralight canoe could be the best way to move around the city.

Navigating up or down rivers can get you away from disaster and danger areas easier than trying to use many other vehicles.

In some cases with a water-bottle purifier, allows the boater to dip and drink on the go.

If you are in crocodile waters, no type of boat, inflatable boat, or small canoe is safe unless it is very big. There are cases where crocodiles have attacked canoes.

Struggling with the wind for sure will tire you out. The wind will tip a canoe easier. Position yourself at angles to the wind to avoid this. Make sure you are paddling on the opposed side as your partner, rotating occasionally. A canoe is more stable and harder than a kayak.

Pros

A canoe doesn't run out of gas.

You can go where no other boat can.

In weed-filled waterways, a canoe can move in a few inches of water.

More strong than kayaks.

They are simpler to go into and properly exit.

With the extra space, you can carry a lot more gear.

Cons

The need to learn paddle strokes to control them

Less efficient than kayaks

Reaching over the side and moving the center balance too far on one side will cause the canoe to flip.

Kayak

A kayak has the advantage of being lighter than a canoe. In a kayak, the paddler is seated and makes use of a double-blade paddle to pull the water on each side to move forward. In a canoe, the paddler operates a single-blade paddle to thrust the boat forward.

Pros

| Kayak don't capsize easily | They are faster than canoes. | More maneuverable on the water |

Cons

Kayaks offer less space than canoes.
More difficult to enter and exit

Walking

Going by foot is preferred when cars, scooters, motorcycles, and bikes become a liability because you can move quietly and hide more easily.

Remove and don't take with you anything that would show where your home is located. If you have to abandon your vehicle, the last thing you want is for those who find it to know where you and your group live.

No matter which vehicle you decide to use, here is a short example of what you should take with you.

Extra-cold clothing: extra pairs of socks

Medical kit: tampons (if necessary)

Some food, water, and a two-way radio

Gas mask with cartridges

Maps, a small tool kit, a flashlight, and a fixed-blade knife

Sidearm Firearm: Sidearm Ammunition

Lesson 8

Drones

This book won't be complete, if I don't mention drones. There will be different crisis situations: maybe a government coup, an invasion, or a tyrannical government martial law.

You have to assume there will be surveillance drones; Anyway, the basics you can do are to take advantage of the natural environment. One of the best things you can do is wait for bad weather. Small to medium drones have a hard time flying in high winds, dense fog, and heavy rain.

Another idea you can do is confuse a drone by placing mirrors on the ground over broken glass, so the image gets diffuse, bright, and out of focus. Also, if you have to move, try to travel in dense areas of foliage, walk close to buildings, and wear a cap, sunglasses, and a wig.

How to plan a cross-country trip after the SHTF

It is going to be very dangerous to take a long trip after SHTF. The first step to safe travel is to outline your route before going out, which includes the roads you will take to reach your destination as well as many backup routes if your first route becomes frightful.

How far are you traveling? Just across town? All the way outside the state? Do you know where you are going to stop to rest for a few hours? For a few days? Do you know if this spot is safe?

You must pay attention to the weather. It can significantly affect your travel, so you must be prepared for harsh weather conditions. Weather conditions are vital to traveling long distances after the SHTF, if you can do it at all.

You may be stranded in the snow, dirt, or sand, but at the same time, you must be invisible to gangs and thieves, which is very hard to do under these circumstances.

You will face danger every turn you take.

The highway is going to be blocked with stalled cars and trucks; several may have run out of gas; others were assaulted by thugs trying to steal provisions, vehicles, motorcycles, and gas; some even tried to apprehend women.

Keep away from main roads and open areas. Pick isolated roads for safety. Most likely, exits on the highways will be blocked, so you must elude them.

If the government is still in control somehow, there will be martial law, and the army will have checkpoints on all highways.

If you are determined to go on a long trip, you will have to stop to rest and sleep. Totally camouflage your vehicle while at rest. If you are on the road with another person, one should stay on guard all the time.

If you must spend the night in your vehicle, look for locations that are hard to see, like threes for natural covers. Nonetheless, you don't want to stop too far from your planned route. Be prepared to flee at a moment's notice if you encounter dangerous people.

There are only three vehicles you can use:

A bicycle, motorcycle, or pickup truck.

A bicycle will take you forever to reach your destination if it is far away, and you will be too slow to escape if you are attacked by thugs.

You could also be riding between stranded cars when someone jumps out from behind them and knocks you off with a wood stick or pipe, steals your bike and supplies, and probably kills you.

A pick-up truck will use a lot of gas; in a SHTF situation, gas will be scarce, even if you collect some.

Are you planning to stay or do a roundtrip? You have to keep in mind that there will be many detours, you may be forced to take alternative streets, gangs will see you coming from far away, and if you have to hide the truck, it will be almost impossible to do it.

The motorcycle will be the better option; it uses much less gas, in case you have to escape from an attack; it is fast; you could take backroads, alleys, and short cuts through grass; even though train rails if are nearby, you could hide it easily if you have to.

Frank Marchante

One inconvenience is that someone can shoot you from far.

It is not wise to make such a trip, at least in the first 8 or 9 months after the SHTF.

If, for some personal reason, you must do this excursion, you should study all the alternatives, routes, weather and personal safety before deciding on such a dangerous mission.

Also, you should try to listen to a ham radio operator that transmits close to the area you are trying to visit to find out the condition of the terrain and weather before you decide to go.

If you need to fire your weapon for whatever reason, move out right away; your location will have been jeopardized.

You must also plan how much gas you will need to take for the roundtrip if you are planning to come back.

You also need to take some water, emergency canned food, some oil, and a spare tire. You don't know how or what situation you are going to face. You must realize that you may lose your life on this journey.

What you should take with you if you decide to take this trip

In your person:

Helmet: to protect the head from rocks or similar objects

Backpack	Maps
Light binocular	Lighter
Blade knife	Tactical flashlight

Side-arm pistol in a holster with a 3-bullet magazine

Or revolver with a three-speed loader

In your backpack:

Kleenex is also used as toilet paper

Tampons, if necessary

First aid kit	Two-way radio
Insect repellant	I sweater
1 pant	1 shirt
2 under ware	2 pairs of socks
1Siphon	1 N95 dust mask
1 tool kit	1oil can

Bikes attach:

5 gallons of gas, Jerry can fuel, back-up fuel emergency

AR-15, shotgun or rifle	Small, light sleeping pad	Spare tire

Lesson 9

Specific survival weapons

Prepare to protect yourself

Weapons, especially guns, rifles and ammo, are going to be high on the list of items to steal. You'll want to carry some other form of self-defense; you won't want to waste bullets unnecessary. A gear is only valuable if you know how to use it.

Alternatives firearms in a SHTF situation

There are many alternatives to firearms, in a SHTF situation you have to do with whatever weapon you have. Alternatives are slingshots, bows and arrows, crossbows, spears, traps and snares.

The AR-15 is the top famous rifle in America, and it is supposed to be easy to obtain parts while foraging.

AR-15 is excellent for self-defense, they are accurate, reliable and simple to use.

The AR-15 need to be kept reasonable clean and well lubricated.

Most AR15 are chambered in 5.56 NATO but almost all are capable of shooting Remington 223 as well. The rule is ok to shoot 223 in a 5.56 gun, but is not ok to shoot 5.56 in a 223 gun.

.22 rifles it is an excellent light weight caliber for hunting small game. It's controversial when it comes to use in self-defense. You can carry many rounds in a backpack.

It is capable of killing humans; it has been used by assassin, and criminals.

The real benefits to .22 LR, though, are small size, light weight, the Ammo is easy to store and carried, and relatively quiet.

Marlin Model.22 LR1895 Rifle

AK- 47 is durable and rugged can run thousands of round without being cleaned, and is also used by military police.

Is AK-47 better than AR15? AR15-rifle is lighter and has a better rate of accuracy.

The problem with the AK-47 for a SHTF is the availability of the ammunition. After the apocalypse all the AK-47 imports of ammo will stop, making very hard to find while scavenging.

Automatic Pistols-The biggest benefit of semi-automatic pistols are high capacity, some have 17+ round capacities, and another benefit of a semi-automatic pistol in self-defense is the ability to load a new magazine quickly. Most of the triggers in a semi-auto are easier to manipulate.

If you go hand-to-hand combat with a human, it's all too easy for the magazine release to get depressed.

For infrequent shooters, it's hard to remember how an automatic pistol operates. A gun you fumble to operate will do you no good, if a youngsters or an old person need to defend themselves with an automatic pistol they have not used for years, they won't remember how to clear a jam, or how to slide the slide, or which button release the magazine.

9mm Luger pistol- it offers greater magazine capacity, 9mm is a powerful, high-velocity round with low recoil, good accuracy and compact dimensions, that you can fit in an pocket.

This caliber is among the best suited for older shooters for personal defense. Ammo is popular, and readily available, so it won't be very hard to find some. Good handgun to have after the apocalypse.

Double action revolvers-popular choice-the hammer is internal or concealed, all you have to do is pull the trigger. You will never lose a magazine with a revolver.

Double action revolver doesn't have a slide to pull back, or a magazine to change.

They are much less susceptible to malfunctions and jams than semi-automatic pistol.

Revolvers are simpler mechanically than semi-automatic handguns, with a lowered risk of the firearm malfunction. Also they are easier to clean than semi-automatic pistol.

357 magnum revolver you can shoot a 357, 38 special, 38 and 38+P. All of these different ammo in just one gun, the 357 Magnum.

Revolver .38 Special- Has enough power to stop a violent attack. Are rugged and simple, the advantage is not requiring a magazine, and the disadvantage is limited capacity and slower reloading. It's ideal for concealed carry.

Known for accuracy and manageable recoil, one of the most popular revolver cartridges in the world. It is small, light and simple to operate. In reality a four-inch barrel revolver may be fed heavy loads offering excellent wound capability.

The snub-nose .38 is also a good defensive firearm.

Pump Shotgun- The shotgun is certainly the most versatile, reliable, and simple firearm in the world. One of the most crucial firearms to have while the SHTF.

The shotgun is a proven trench fighter and (if need be) will drop larger animals.

The idea behind possessing a shotgun is for actions and conflicts of short duration at close range. There no other firearms quite as efficient as a shotgun at close range.

Maverick 12 Gauge tactical shotgun

Shotgun shells come in all types for different purpose. Some are designed to hunt small game such as bird or rabbit. You will need something like buckshot necessary for any animal over 50 pounds and great for personal defense.

Shotguns also can be used for breaching doorways to benefit access into locked rooms or buildings. The advantage to the shotgun is the hitting power.

The exceptional preference for city survival, *Double barrel shotgun*
Shotgun is made through Remington or Mossberg.
They are utilized by each police and navy forces across the world.

The most common are Buckshot for hunting, Slugs are use to hunt deer. Most shotguns are chambered in 12, 20, and .410 gauges.

12 gauge-the most popular in the United States. Most 12ga shotguns weight almost twice as 20ga, the recoil is much stronger.

20 gauge-is the next most popular by shooters uncomfortable with the recoil of a 12-gauge gun.

.410 shells- they are smaller and less powerful, however is a formidable threat if you are facing the barrel. It's ideal because can be use by an older person, wife or even youngsters.

0.30-30 Winchester-The .30-30 is a very useful and efficient caliber for protection as well as a game getting. You can use it for patrol, protection and hunting. Is light weight, simple to shoot with relative low recoil.

Universal Safety rules for firearms- also apply for safety at home

Assume all guns are always loaded

Keep finger off the trigger until you fire

Never point a firearm at anything you don't want to shoot

Keep gun or rifle on safe until you fire

Know your backstop

In a SHTF firearms will be essential to protect you, your family, home, food, animal, and as well for hunting animals for food.

Keep your weapons clean

You must find a way to keep your firearms clean and lubricated.

Combat rust- use oil to prevent rust, then you must clean the chamber with a dry patch.

In an emergency you can use new motor oil to oil your gun, this might not be a great option, just keep it in mind.

You can also use 3-1 oil to clean rifle barrel, but is not ideal.

I have never tried it myself, but is good to know in case of an emergency like SHTF situation.

Just be careful, and try it before in a small part of your weapon.

Bulletproof vests

Bulletproof vests- also known as a ballistic vest or a bullet resistant vest, are designed to stop a bullet from penetrating and causing harm to the wearer saving their lives. You should have obtained one before SHTF.

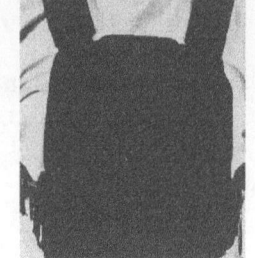

Preferable if possible, every member in your scout team should wear one. It will be impossible to find one after the SHTF.

Here is basic information in some of them.

Cover body armor is meant to be concealed. Usually not as strong as overt body armor. Usually is wear under cloth. They are best when you do not wish to draw attention to your protection.

Overt body armor is much stronger and many can even block bullets from powered rifles. They are bulkier and harder to move when wearing one.

Plate carrier this is another variety of a bulletproof vest, they are lighter and more comfy than the full armor vest. They can be soft or hard armor plate to provide different levels of protection.

Soft Armor plate Soft Armor plate are flexi plate and soft, still strong unusually worn concealed.

Hard Armor plate provides the higher level of protection, not as comfortable as soft armor plate.

The U.S. National Institute of Justice has established unique performance-safety level. Its divide t into 5 different threat levels:

Level 1A---- LEVEL11--- LEVEL111A

LEVEL 111--- LWEVEL 1V

BB Guns

When you talk about a home protection gun, a BB gun does not usually come to mind when considering home protection

More conventional is an actual gun.

Many people think having a BB gun is the perfect choice to a real gun. Of course, it does not have the effectiveness of a real gun has, it still is a valuable defense weapon. The advantage is easy to shoot, no loud muzzle blast, the ammo is extremely light and compact.

BB gun targets are likely to be use for small feather pets such as pigeons, sparrows and crows, or varmints like ground squirrels, raccoon and coyotes.

Break-barrel air weapons require:

A single cocking motion to compress a powerful internal spring. Modern BB guns usually comes with a smoothbore 4.5 barrel (0.177 in)

Small and medium size birds are good targets for .177 caliber air rifles. If you want to hunt bigger birds you need a bigger air rifle.

CO2- BB guns use a small disposable cartridge that allows multiple shots. Not ideal for a SHTF situation when you run out of cartridges

Pellet gun vs BB gun- which one is the best for you?

While BB guns and pellet guns are quite similar in some way, there are also a lot of differences.

Types of pellet guns:

The Multiple pump. Up to 10 cocking motions are required to compress the air in a chambered.

Differences between a BB gun and a pellet gun:

BB guns and pellets guns differ in a multiple ways when it comes to ammunition, design and accuracy.

The biggest difference between BB guns and pellets guns is the ammo used in them. BB ammunitions are small, round steel balls. They come in different construction materials.

Pellets ammunition is available in distinct shapes and sizes; they may be Wadcutter pellets, pointed pellets, hollow pellets, and hybrid pellets.

The mag utilized in pellets weapons isn't like a BBs. BBs are smooth to stack them collectively within inside the mag, normally preserve lots extra ammo of their mag than pellet gun. This so not possible for pellets guns.

If you need more hunting capabilities and extra power, you ought to go for a pellet gun. Both BB guns and pellets gun can cause serious injury; even can kill a person if a person is shoot in close range.

BB weapons and pellets weapons are each supplied in C02 models. CO2 guns use a small disposable cartridge that allows multiple shots. Not ideal for a SHTF situation when you run out of cartridges.

Slingshots

Slingshots are highly portable and light weight. They can be extremely effective on small game.

You may use steel ball bearings, or Glass marbles, you can even use small pebbles in an emergency. You can place a small sling into a backpack or even your pocket, but they are also a formidable hunting firearm that can be used to kill small game like squirrel, rabbits, geese and ducks. You can also carve one and make one from a tree branch in an emergency.

Test the band condition of your band Regularly so it can be ready. Slingshots ought to be used at brief distance.

The author practicing

Wood slingshots- if you do build one from a tree branch keep close caution for crack in the wood fork.

It's a great idea to get some training to use a slingshot, 33 feet is the encourage distance to practice. It will take a lot of practice to become proficient.

Aiming is done by holding the slingshot at an angle and using the tip of the upper arm of the Y as your sight.

Disadvantage you can only shoot one at the time.

The Bow

A bow is quiet and depending in your choice of arrows, can be used to hunt small game, big game, birds and even fish. Long bows and recurves are traditional and have less that can go wrong.

Survival experts recommend the simpler bows than the modern one complicated pulley system. Downside when carrying them in a thick bush can be problematic.

Author with a homemade Bow

Advantages:

Almost silent   Often reusable   You can craft your own ammo

Crossbow

The crossbow excels as both a defense weapon and a hunting weapon. A light weigh crossbow may be easier to Carrie.

You don't run out of ammo, as long as you recover your arrows, with proper care and maintained can last for years.

Crossbows are extremely popular because you can fire them like a rifle.

There are configurations of arrowheads:

Points and Broadheads
Points like bullets and field tips are used for small game.
Broaheads are used for big game.

Arrowheads can be made of various materials. Draw weight-is how much force it takes to fully pull back the bowstring.

Machetes, and knifes

The Machete

It's lethal, and it comes in just about every shape, style and size imaginable. However, they take considerable skill to use it effectively. You would do with machete  anything you can do with a Hatched, but it will be lighter and won't use any room in your pack if you choose one with a blade of about 18 to 22 inches long. The machete is an essential one large blade with a handle, it's critical that the blade extend all way to the very bottom of the handle.

A machete built like this is said to be full tang machete. Few tools have the ability to chop down a small three just as fast scare off intruders. The Machete is call "insane versatility".

Knifes blades

Below are the most common types of steel use to make knifes blades.

Carbon Steel-extremely strong, it holds a decent edge, but rust if you don't take care for it.

Stainless Steel-Wont rust or corrode, comes in a huge variety of grades.

Titanium- Very popular with scuba diving, Titanium is very strong rust resistant material.

High Carbon Stainless Steel-The advantage are that it doesn't rust.

Most survival knives blades will be either a grade of Stainless Steel or a specific type of carbon steel.

What is a Tactical knife?

A tactical knife is a knife that is designed with more than one function or feature.

What is a complete tang knife?

Full tang means that the blade extends the full length of the grip.

Fixed blades knives-The fixed blade is strong and durable.

Hunting and camping knifes-The best use for hunting knives includes skinning, boning, gutting.

Solid Pommel-Is the handle's butt end. Survival knives feature a hollow handle for storing matches, etc.

Stainless Steel and high carbon metals are the most popular choices for blade manufacturing. You also find specialty knives with Titanium or even ceramic blades.

Knifes handles

Below are some popular choices for knives handle:

Wood-Hardwood is superior to softwood. A high quality wood is extremely durable.

 Horn-Knifes handles made from antler are very popular.

ABS- Basically a type of plastic. It's tough and designed for hard frequent use. Be careful with the grip as you can lose grip in wet conditions.

Bone-This bone handle could come from any critter. The surface is roughed up to provide a sure grip. Bone can be dyed in almost any color.

Paracord -_Some full-tang knives have their handles wrapped in military grade 550 Paracord. This gives a good grip and provides additional features length of Paracord at your disposable.

Clipping a knife to a pocket at the sturdy facet also can be a powerful location, as you may put on a sheathed knife on a series round your neck.

Tomahawk- Hatchet-and Ax

Difference between a tomahawk and a hatchet- is that a Tomahawk is a long-handed ax with a shorter, narrower blade and a straight wooden shaft. It contain a very thin blade that is lightweight, are most used in ax-throwing, hunting and self-defense.

The hatched is more compact and has a short handle, and also has a heavy blade on the head. A small handle and a sharp, thick head is the key to identifying a hatched.

AXE- Also spelled Axe, you can use an axe to cut wood, and branches, you can not only use it as a tool, but also as a weapon, an axe can save your life.

Spear

A spear is a pole weapon made of a shaft with a pointed head, usually made of wood. Spears are divided in two kinds, thrusting and ranged weapon. The American Indians used the spear for hunting, fishing and combat. Along other weapons the spear is one of the earliest and most important tool develops by early humans.

Items that can be use as defense:

Flare guns-Flare guns could be used as a weapon. Particularly against animals.

Launching flares can be an effective deterrent against a charging bear or moose.

A flare gun could be the only thing between you and a life-threatening gang member.

Under U.S. Federal law, flare gun are not classified under firearms category per se. However stats and local government may have different perspective. Under A SHTF I don't think anybody will mind.

There have been many cases of flare guns being at the heart of devastating house and forest fire across the U.S. Keep this in mind and be caution.

Expired flares may still work as long as they have been stored correctly and safely.

Blackjack

The sap, slapper or blackjack is a heavy pouch, eight to twelve inches long, filled with lead and sometimes with smell pieces of rock. Its size and shape allowed to be concealed on a pocket.

One of the best uses of the blackjack in self-defense is attacking a limb reducing the ability of the arm to strike you or immobilizing the attacker by hitting his knee. Striking the temple or the face will easily break the thinner bones inflicting a concussion.

Baton-A baton is a versatile tool, including for self-defense.

Umbrella You can use an umbrella as a club to hit an attacker.

Keys-keys improvised self-dense weapon in a close fight.

Stick- walking stick can be a great self-defense tool.

Hammer-You can use it to break locks, rescue people from inside rooms. Very useful and handy in a survival situation. It is highly portable and very handy in a close-up fight,

Black Jack club- a small wooden club about 15 inches long, most of the time is crafted from wood with a strength-wrap handle.

Brass knuckles-These portions of metallic or maybe polymer may be carried in a pocket to deliver a knock out pressure punch.

Pant Belts- As a defensive weapon, a belt is pretty versatile. You can use it to strike an attacker or as a restraint.

Flashlights-You can use a flashlight as a blunt instrument, like hitting the head, or the nose; a strong hit can kill somebody.

Smoke grenades- Generally speaking, smoke grenades are safe to use near people. Can help you by distracting and obstructing your enemies view, and offer enough time to scape.

In the U.S., smoke grenades are legal in all states. All national parks in the U.S. strictly prohibit the use of smoke grenades due to the threat of fire.

Fire extinguishers as a weapon

In a time of extraordinary need for self-defense, extinguishers can be used with good type degrees of success. As a last ditch defense, including in your home, when there is nothing else available.

Here are the simple kinds of extinguisher you're probable to come upon, and a few protection considerations. Not all fire extinguish are ideal for work as a self-defense tool.

Class A-These are maximum use on fires such as wood, paper, fabric, plastic or trash.

Class B- Use for fires that use flammable liquid includes, gasoline, kerosene, oils, or oil based paints.

Class C –Electrical fires. This class of fire extinguisher is good for components as a fuel source. Can be as a result of overloading wiring or circuits.

Class K-Theses are usually used for cooking fires and are intended to put out fires that utilize a variety of materials as fuel.

Cooking oil to vegetable fats can be extinguished utilizing a Class K for this kind of fire. If you utilize the incorrect extinguish you run the danger of spreading the fire.

ABC Powder Extinguisher

These compact, hand held multi-purpose fire extinguish are extremely popular today. This powder covers the fire and put it out. As a self-protection, you'll discover ABC energy extinguishes exceptional to apply in domestic and public locations as a self-protection tool.

The high pressure discharged by these fire extinguishers can be sufficient to slow down, stop, or disable active shooters, or criminals.

You need to spray the felon until the canister is empty, after which beat them with the empty cylinder.

If the fire extinguisher was used very close to the thug face, it is probable he will be momentarily or permanently blinded.

Steps to use a fire extinguisher

Pull the pin with the extinguisher nozzle aiming far from you, loose the locking mechanism.

Aim low the extinguisher at the attacker.

Squeeze the lever evenly and slowly.

Sweep the nozzle from top to bottom of the attacker body.

Remove your clothing that has residue from the extinguisher on them.

Flush your eyes with running water if any got into your eyes.

Inhalation

If some of the fire extinguishers active agents are inhaled, everyone in the room should got outside right away and get fresh air. Including the aggressor.

Lubrication

Keep all rifles and guns proper lubricated. The biggest enemies of a gun or rifle are rust, oxidation and corrosion. You should maintain your firearm and keep it lubricated to avoid malfunctions.

Magazine maintenance involves inspecting and occasionally removing lint and debris. You also should practice firing with either hand. This may prove to be a lifesaving skill.

Gun handling

Threat every firearms as if it were loaded, this rule is important for your safety and the safety around you.

Always keep you gun pointed in a safe direction. This is the most basic safety rule that you and your team must follow.

The saying is never point a gun at anything you do not intent to shoot. The safest position is to point it down.

Always be certain of what is behind your target.

Author younger years

Safely store a gun

Safe gun save is one of the most needed decisions a gun homeowners can make.

"Extinction is the rule. Survival is the exception"
Carl Sagan

Lesson 10

Water

During a long-term disaster, there is a chance that the water will stop and you won't be able to flush your toilet. Toilets take a few gallons of water to flush; you could haul enough water back home so everybody can flush when they do number 2. You will need to do it on a daily basis

Solar water disinfection:

This is a simple method that uses the UV radiation of the sun to kill harmful pathogens. You place a polyethylene bottle with a cap in sunlight; the sun's UV rays penetrate the water, destroying any harmful pathogens.

To work effectively, the bottles must be clear, not tinted or frosted, and you must remove all labels and stickers. They should also be clean and never have been used to store or clean any potentially harmful substance. Lay the bottles flat so the sun can penetrate the full depth of the water. After about 6 hours of sun exposure, the SODIS process is complete.

Rainwater collection system:

Learning how to gather a sustainable supply of drinking water is an important survival skill. A rain barrel is an easy choice you could use to collect as much water as you can from the rain falling from the sky.

A rain barrel is an easy alternative to a water collection system. Invest in some 5-gallon rain barrels or improvise one yourself. A typical rain barrel holds around 50 gallons of water. You have to clear out and purify any rainwater for cooking or consumption intake from your roof.

It is a great way to capture water and have it filter or clean later.

You can install the barrel under a gutter's downspout to collect rainwater coming off your roof. It is preferable to install the barrel on a surface of concrete or stones to help ensure stability since 55 gallons of rainwater can weigh nearly 500 lbs. combined.

Precaution:

If you live in a climate that gets freezing temperatures in the winter, it's better to drain your water barrel for the season to keep the water from freezing, swelling, and destroying the barrel.

You can chemically disinfect suspect water by using kitchen bleach or maybe swimming pool chlorine; just dilute it enough and make sure that there aren't any other additives like fungicides. Just a few drops of a 5% liquid solution that has sodium hypochlorite index as the principal active ingredient will disinfect a liter of water in an hour.

To filter pool water for drinking, fill a large 55-gallon drum with alternating layers of sand and charcoal. Drill a drainage hole in the bottom, and you can run the water through this filter to get rid of the chlorine.

Items you will regret not having when SHTF

It is very important to keep manuals in a water-resistant case that identify parts and part replacement.

If, post-disaster, you temporarily forget a procedure, for example, how to take a part to clean a firearm you haven't used for a long time, these manuals will help in the future.

Keep a couple of first aid books and some survival manuals like the one you are reading now

Survival Checklist:

Medical supplies

Tools-basic tools

Rain gear or a poncho to keep you dry

Shoes, boots, sneakers, and plenty of socks

Toiletries, toilet paper, and portable toilets

Gardening basics-tools

Gloves-garden and heavy rubber gloves

Nylon cordage is a valuable tool in an improvised situation

Box cutters and utility knives

Tactical Flashlight, Compass, and Topographic Maps

Water filters and water quality test kit

Ammo:

Even if you are against guns, you need them if you want to protect yourself and your family in SHTF circumstances. It would be a good idea to stockpile ammo if you want to defend your family. Also, it is beneficial to stockpile arrowheads and bows just in case.

Lipstick:

Lipstick is a good Firestarter if the main ingredient is petroleum. You can also use it to waterproof small items, as sunscreen, and as an excellent way to write a waterproof message on any surface.

Canned food expiration date:

If your canned food has an expiration date, just open it up; if it smells good and is not rancid, just forget about it and eat it up.

Prisoners in SHTF

There are policies in place and a set of rules for moving prisoners to better facilities in better areas in a crisis. Every state and every jail have written catastrophe emergency plans. The problem is an extremely high collapse. Who is going to apply it? Guards are going to go home to try to save their loved ones; I don't blame them. It is only natural to do so.

In a SHTF scenario, odds are that prisoners will be deserted, or some may escape if they can. Many, of course, will eventually flee into the local area, creating chaos, in search of water, food, liquor, medicine, clothing, and women.

Most criminals have criminal minds; they are always looking for weakness; they will bring violence and abuse; and they will be ruthless.

Some loose prisoners will create their own gangs. Families in the area with this scenario will find it very hard and almost impossible to survive in a SHTF.

Health

This is the most important way to survive the end of the world. You are going to be without access to reliable health care.

First aid:

In a catastrophic world scenario. You might not have access to a doctor or nurse. Store supplies and have books of first aid.

Keep your hands clean. Reports claim that an average person touches his face about 20,000 times a day. Washing your hands is the best way to avoid contracting a virus. In a SHTF situation, if there is no soap, you can also use vinegar or diluted bleach. Be careful if you have to use bleach.

Times you must clean your hands:

Before touching your nose, mouth, and eyes

After taking care of someone sick

When cooking food

After using the toilet

After handling trash

After touching animals

Washing your hair

You can use products like baking soda, apple cider vinegar, and a brush; comb your hair daily if you don't have any shampoo to use.

Vodka uses:

Vodka can be used for a variety of ailments, such as treating cuts, scrapes, sunburns, and toothaches.

Natural remedies to get rid of pinworms:

Consume 3–4 large cloves, first chopping them up, mixed with water, and take one glass four times each day.

Garlic has been used as an antibiotic and antifungal for centuries.

Apple cider vinegar, pumpkin seed oil, and coconut oil have been helpful in getting rid of pinworms.

Keep yourself clean to have a better chance of avoiding reinfection.

Antibiotic

There are two basic categories of antibiotics: broad-spectrum and narrow-spectrum antibiotics. Broad-spectrum antibiotics kill the most forms of bacteria.

Types of bleeding

In general, all major hemorrhages are serious, but many are lethal more rapidly than others.

Someone bleeding profusely can bleed to death in minutes.

Arterial bleeds are the most dangerous because they can cause your heart to push out all the blood.

Capillary: the small blood vessels near the surface of your skin are called capillaries. Unless you have hemophilia, a capillary bleed is rarely a life-threatening event.

If you sliced yourself with your own knife, the first thing to do is stop the bleeding.

The first step if somebody is bleeding

Sit the victim down and apply direct pressure to the wound. This cuts off the blood and gives you time to dress the wound.

Tourniquet

You can make one yourself. A rope is good, as is a bandana or a piece of clothing. Tie it into a square knot. Then use a branch under the tourniquet. The place to apply the tourniquet is very high on the limb. We now know your limb can survive without blood for up to 6 hours. It may even be safer to leave it on for longer because it's better to lose a limb than lose your life.

You should not use a tourniquet on the torso or neck.

How to monitor the wound for infection:

Look for signs of redness, swelling, pus, and pain at the injury site.

Treatment if you suspect an infection:

Soak the injury in water 2 or 3 times a day.

You must make the wound easily reachable; if the edges of the wound are close together, pull them apart. Apply an antibiotic, or anything similar available.

Clean, irrigate, and dry the wound again.

Monitor signs and symptoms.

Lesson 11

Refrigeration

In America, 99.8% of all homes contain one refrigerator. Certain medicines, like insulin, must be kept cold to extend their lives and potency.

Until refrigerators were common in America, root cellars were the way families kept their food for the winter, from the 18th century through the early 20th century.

The root cellar was a typical below-ground excavation located close to the house.

Bucket as a root cellar

Buried in a five-gallon bucket, either a metal or plastic one with a lid, most people prefer plastic since metal can rust. Drill holes in the bottom, dig a large hole, and place the bucket upright in the hole. Fill in the area around the bucket with dirt. Close the bucket with the lid and cover the entire area with a tarp.

Foods that need to be sore at 40 or below:

Meat, poultry, seafood, and dairy products: cooked food

Foods that can be kept at room temperature:

Canned food-Honey-Bread-Dried beans, rice, pasta-Coffee Butter-Tomatoes-Bananas-Potatoes.

Zeer pot

Zeer pot, also known as a pot-in refrigerator, is a simple primitive way to keep your food cold. Zeer pot is still used in many regions of the world.

A zeer is constructed by placing a clay pot in a larger clay pot with wet sand in between the pots and a wet cloth on top. You place the food in the inner pot to prevent the penetration of liquid. The evaporation of the outer pot draws heat from the inner pot.

It cools as the water evaporates, allowing refrigeration in hot, dry climates. These devices tend to perform poorly in climates with high ambient humidity.

When done properly, it can extend the shelf life of food by 5 to 10 times compared to room-temperature storage. Do not place milk or leftovers in the pot.

Outcomes:

Keeps food cool.
Keeps insects away.

Flaws:

Foods must be checked frequently.
Ensure the internal temperature is at a consistent temperature.

Cooking

Finding ways to cook without smelling the food will be one of your biggest problems. You will need to find ways to be able to cook and heat your home with no noise or bright light without attracting unnecessary attention.

An earth oven, floor oven, or cooking pit is one of the best and most historic cooking structures. An earth oven is a pit within the floor used to trap heat and bake or steam food. The earth oven nevertheless continues to be a common tool for cooking large amounts of food where no equipment is accessible.

To construct an amazing cooking pit, use blocks or stones stacked at least 2 feet from the ground. Excavate a pit a foot or so deep so that you have sufficient space.

A practical way to cook bigger foods like chunks of meat or entire small game is to roast them on a spit over an open fire.

Methods of cooking:

Baking involves applying dry convection heat to your food in an enclosed environment.

Frying means cooking your food in fat.

Roasting: This method of cooking is a very effective way to cook; all you need is a fire and a stick; it is also the safest method as well.

Grilling: this is an emergency cooking method that uses coal or wood. Place food over an open fire and cook.

Steaming: by boiling water into steam, the steam transmits heat to the food, thus cooking it.

Poaching: heating food submerged in a liquid such as water
Simmering: This method brings the liquid below the boiling point over lower heat.

Broiling: is similar to grilling, except the heat comes from above instead of bellow.

Rock cooking

An alternative choice for food preparation over an open fire is to use a large rock. Just prop a wide, flat rock over the fire. It will get hot, and you can put your pot or pan right on it.

How to build a mud oven:

Obtain a clay pod or metal, with a lid.

Dig a ditch in firm mud about one or two foot deep.

Place the cooking pot on its side over one end of the ditch.

Place a long, thick stick vertically nearby the bottom end of the cooking pod.

Pack mud firmly around pod. Make sure the stick still protrudes from the top of the stack.

Remove the stick to create a chimney, the hole will allow stream and smoke to escape from underneath the pot.

Build a fire below the cooking pod; feed the flame with wood until the sparks glow brightly.

Place your food inside the pot. Cover the food in thick leaves to keep it clean from mud and dirt.

Use a stick to hold up the lid against the opening of the oven. If you close the opening it will enhance cooking effectiveness.

Feed the fire as needed until the food has finished cooking.

Hobo Stove

A very basic and simple stove made from tin cans and fueled by sticks, twigs, etc. This design can be made from supplies that most people have on hand. A benefit of leaving the bottom of your hobo stove open is that it's easier to create a fire in it. You can start the fire outside of the stove, get it going, and then set up the hobo stove.

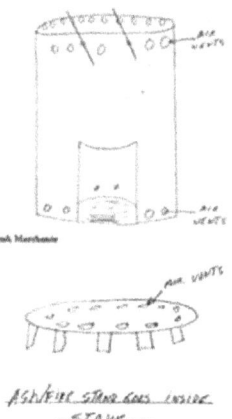

Basic Hobo Stove:
Decide which side will be up.

Punch flame holes, make a pot stand, and you will need to punch some holes to allow flames through.

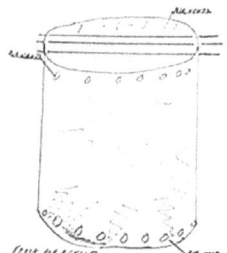

Create air vents.
Cook out door
Open fire

This is the most primitive way of cooking, and it may be the most practical way of cooking.

Open fires allow for several cooking options: pans can be placed directly in the fire, rested on hot embers; food can be covered in aluminum foil and positioned near the fire.

Camp stoves run off of a small bottle of gas, which is nice as long as you have a gas bottle.

Dehydrating food

The easiest way is through sun dehydration (sun drying). You lay your food out and let the sun suck out the moisture. Low moisture preserves the food, helping it last longer. You can also dry food by letting it slowly bake over a heat source, like a campfire, until crisp.

Remember that eating undercooked food can be dangerous, so make sure it is cooked through. To avoid getting sick.

Safety

Grills should always be used outdoors and at a safe distance from your home or shelter. Carbon monoxide can be deadly. The same goes for a camp stove or a fireplace.

Never use treated wood for food preparation, as the chemicals can get into your food.

Never use gasoline to get a fire going.

Never leave a fire without an adult around to keep an eye on it.

Remove any trash from around the campfire. Use caution when handling or moving items containing hot pots. Loose clothing, like long sleeves is also risky; fabrics can melt fast when a spark hits them. There should always be a shovel and a bucket of water in case a fire gets out of control.

Keep Those Flames at Bay

Large quantities of salt can put out fires. If you have a fireplace, you can extinguish the flames by pouring salt on them.

If you ever face a grease fire, in the place of water pour salt on it. Putting water will only expand the oil, in so doing spreading the fire. You can use salt or baking soda to lower rogue fires on a grill or frying pan.

Food

Four Condition that affect food storage

Condition #1-Temperature to keep well dried food for longer time

Condition #2-How food are store-food packed in air do not store well, better to store in oxygen.

Condition #3-What you use to store in-must has an air tight seal

Dairy Dehydrate products are better store if stored dry hermetically in seal containers.

Condition #4-Prepare a storage space for short term and long term food storage.

Storage is a challenge if you are working with a small space.

Canned food last many years

Canned food will last for years, as long as the can itself is in good condition (no rust, dents, or swelling).

Package foods (cereal, pasta, cookies) will be safe past the best by date; they may eventually become stale or develop an off flavor.

Grain, Rice, and Beans

What foods should you store for a long time? Rice and grain are so important for long term food storage.

If you had to, you could survive on theses food alone for an extended period of time. When store properly you are looking at a 30 years shelf life.

Rice can last around five years and up to thirty years if you keep it in an oxygen-free container. You and your family can survive on two small bowls of rice a day, for a long time if necessary.

Potato flakes

Good survival food fast supply is potato flakes. Add boiling water and within minutes dinner is served. Also can be used to make thin soups and gravies. Potato flakes are ideal for 25-30 years storage.

Baking Soda.

Baking soda can be used as a leaving agent, for cleaning, for personal hygiene, and for medical purposes. It has an indefinite shelf life and is inexpensive, store as many as you can.

Apple cider

Vinegar is known for its medicinal properties. Vinegar is important as a cleaner and disinfectant. Vinegar can be stored forever in the right container. Over time vinegar will eat through plastic.

The best containers for long-term are glass.

Eggs are an excellent protein source, and they provide fat, most Americans have difficulty slaughtering animals.

Here is a list to storage:

Dried beans	Pasta
Grains like Wheat	Dehydrated Foods
Instant potatoes salt	Freeze-foods
Sugar	Dried Lentils
Low fat powered milk	Powered Eggs

Keep temperature food.

Honey	Coffee
Unopened canned food	Bread
Dried beans, rice, pasta	Butter
Tomatoes	Potatoes
Bananas	Winter Squash

Sand to keep food cool.

Many root veggies may be saved in sand for months with no refrigeration.

Such as: carrots, beets, turnips, potatoes, parsnips, ginger and more.

Storing root vegetables in sand helps keep the moisture, air and humidity at the right temperature to prevent ripening and rotting.

Vegetable garden.

Starting your own garden is a must for you and your family survival, there won't be more stores for you to buy food. However, building a productive garden takes years.

Vegetables easily produced include:

Tomatoes	Lettuce
Zucchini squash.	Beets
Cabbage	Chard
Bush beans	Carrots

Top seven healthier fruits:

Apple-A low calorie snack high in both soluble and insoluble fiber.

Banana	Grapes
Citrus fruit.	Papaya
Coconut	Pineapple

Salt:

Using salt as food preservative will keep your food lasting longer, you can use salt to dry meats so they will last longer and will not spoil. You must try to find and stock up on as much quantity as possible.

Chicken:

Can provide both meat and fresh eggs, keeping a hen for eggs is a great idea.

Tin can remove:

Grind the top of the can in a flat circle way pushing down onto a paving slab. You'll quickly wear away the thin metal lip and get that lid off.

According to the Mayo Clinic, food poisoning symptoms can be:

Nausea	Abdominal pain
Vomiting	Fever
Watery or bloody diarrhea	

As much as possible, stick to canned foods prepared for long-term storage. In order to be on the safe side as possible as relates to spoilage. In most cases, potato chips last about 2 or 3 months, but if the bag stays closed and it's kept in a dark, cool, and dry place, they could last well over a year.

Dark chocolate could last for up to 5 years if you were to keep it at a fairly constant temperature of about 65 °F.

Energy Bar

From the moment they're manufactured, these bars usually don't expire for about 3 years, etc., if it expires, you can still eat them for another year.

Twinkies

They also have the potential to last for up to 30 years.

Food companies:

There are many companies for emergency long term foods.

Popular options for long-term food companies are:

Mountain House, My patriot supply, Legacy food, ReadyWise food. Meal ready to eat (MREs) are sold to Americans who wants to storage supplies for any emergency circumstances.

Gather a useful group as you can, at least place somebody in your home or group into these categories as possible.

Doctor/nurse-to cure illness or infection.

Hunter-To hunt animals and butcher the animal they hunt.

Military police-to protect and to combat predators

Teachers-or someone to teach the kids, the next generation.

Cook-to prepares food and ration food properly.

Builder-to fix basic structures.

Mechanic-repair devices and vehicles

Farmers-to grow and take care of food.

Learn to fish

Even in large cities there are different spots where you can catch fish, from local rivers and streams, to small park and golf course ponds. Fishing can be a totally efficient way to get food.

Loud noises make the fish leave the area. Always stay silent when fishing.

Humans were fishing since the beginning of civilization. Fishing is one of the fine strategies to get protein in a survival situation. Freshwater fish feed on bacteria and they are loaded with it. Never eat raw freshwater fish, it could make you sick.

A simple stick with a line and a hook usually do, there is much easier and better way to catch fish. Fisherman claim that the best time to fish is about 3 hours for the duration of sunrise and sunset on an incoming tide.

This is when fish are looking for food. Fish tend to bite better throughout the day in deeper water.

The most effective way for everyone with no experience to catch fish is by net. You can construct an emergency fishing net with wood branches, and use a piece of cloth tied to two sticks.

Wade through the water, gradually and quietly, in direction of the shore. When you get to shallow water, lift the net to expose your catch.

To preserve your catch, you should put the fish in your cooler immediately after catching it.

You could use for a survival fish hooks a safety pins, or paper clips, a small bone, sharp stick, and you could cut a soda can and make a hook out of it.

Finding a bait

You could find something to use as bait around you.

Hand-fishing.

When you don't have any equipment you can try hand fishing. People calling it graveling, or noodling, it is an old fishing system.

It entails grabbing the fish straightway from its hiding spot with your hand. It is more seen when fishing catfish, who like to hide in dark places like hollow logs, undercut banks and holes under the rocks.

Spearfishing:

Spear fishing requires a spear; you can make one from a wooden stick.

Ice Fishing:

If you live in a very cold state-ice fishing is an alternative, there are two ways to catch fish through the ice-ice traps-called tip-ups or use a jigging rod. The best time to ice fish is sunrise and sunset.

For many lakes the better shallow or deep is in the 8 to 20 foot zone, depending on the species.

Ice safe to walk on:

Your number one main concern must always be safety. The truth is ice fishing is never 100 % safe. Ice is secure to stroll on wherein there's four inches or greater of clean ice. It is critical to check ice conditions and thickness to find out if it is safe for ice fishing.

Ice thickness chart:

Less than 4 inches-stay off

4 inches-minimum for ice fishing on foot

5 to 7 inches-one snowmobile or ATV.

8 to 12 inches-one small car or small pick-up

12 to 15 inches-one medium truck

What to do in case you fall in the ice.

Don't remove your winter clothing it will trap air to help you float.

Turn toward the direction you came-probable the strongest ice.

To provide traction to pull yourself up, position your hands and arms on the unbroken ice surface, ice picks or sharpened screwdrivers come very handy for this. Kick your feet in the direction back onto the solid ice.

Lie flat at the ice after you are out and roll far from the hole.

Get to a heated, dry, protected area, to warm up yourself right away, you must try to find medical attention as soon as you can.

Never ice fish alone-never ice fish alone-never ice fish alone

Cleaning the fish:

This is the most unpleasant step in the cooking process. Insert the knife into the belly near the tail , make a cut all the way to the head. Be cautious not to cut the intestine, as the fish there have an unpleasant bitter taste. Gradually opens the body to get the intestine out. Slit the anus. If there is a dark spot adjacent to the backbone, cut it off. Rinse the fish in clean water.

What Looter-criminal and pillager will look for?

Listen for the sounds of tools or engines.

Smell like wood or cooking.

At night they will look for lights.

Maybe a scanner to listen to radio traffic like walkie-talkies.

Optical devices day and night to look further.

Idea:

A shooting and communication platform would be ideal.

Long term:

How are you going to sustain your family in the long term?

Steps to consider:

Rationing food.

First, eat food that needs freezing before going bad.

Think about farming-right away — don't lose time

Winter Rations

Make maps of alternative routes to get passed controlled by violent gangs.

Have and take good care of survival manuals, guns manuals, health medicine manuals, and how to books.

Emergency food shortage:

Families will eat smaller portions

People in emergency will turn to neighbors and family for food

Skip meals once a day-in worst situation will eat meal every other day

If they are lucky and have livestock, they will exchange some for other kind of food

They will be Foraging for foods everywhere

Family will be eating anything there is available

Some will turn to rob, assault or even kill to feed their kids

LESSON 12

Heat

You can keep your home warm in the winter and cooler in the summer by opening and closing windows and shades according to the sun patterns. Feel around your doors and windows for cold drafts and cover them with towels or blankets to keep out the cold air.

Plant and use trees and shrubbery to provide shade to your house or outside kitchen.

If you don't have electricity, you can hang a piece of wet cloth at the front entrance or window that catches a good breeze. You can cool the temperature in the room by several degrees. Keep the curtain closed during the day, to prevent sunlight coming into your home. Cook outside during hot summer days is also a good idea.

Cold home-ways not to freeze in the winter:

You can build or put up a tent inside in your living room or in another room, pack yourself with a heavy coat, socks and a sleeping bag. Various members can sleep inside, probably with body heat.

Block all openings to keep cold air from coming in and conserve heat. Block windows to keep the cold out. Stop drafts, air seeps in through cracks in Windows.

Filling up a woodshed, you will need a lot of cords of wood to make it through the winter. Gathering the wood, splitting and cutting into the right shapes and pieces is a very hard work.

Remember you have to keep it all dry so you can actually use as firewood. Reduce opening doors.

Make sure water in the toilets so don't freeze and crack, if your pipes freeze may burst, make sure it doesn't happen.

Water filter

The tap may still run water but is the water safe? Clean water becomes a lifesaver. Use filters like the LifeStraw Or Sawyer to help clean drinking water, or you have to boiled it to make sure is clean.

Rain collection system

You'll want to set up a simple roof rainwater collection system. You can collect an impressive amount of water if you have barrels on each downspout. In a SHTF situation occurs everyone will start collecting rain water.

How to wash clothes clean

You will need two to five gallon buckets.

One-five gallon bucket Lid

Make many holes thru one of the bucket, drill a hole in the center of the top lid, leave about 1 inch free at the top of the lid. This will gives you room for bubbles to form when you agitated with the plunger, make sure you can fit the plunger thought the top lid and you can push up and down.

Add cloth, add water and fit the lid of the washer on top, so the plunger handle fit thorough the central opening

Push and pull for about 10 minutes, empty out soapy water and refill with clean water. Agitate clothes for another 5 minutes to remove soap and dirt. Do as many times as necessary to remove all soap from your cloth. Once they are clean, remove from bucket with holes, water will drip out thru the holes, and hang clothes to dry.

Soap-making:

Soap can be made from scratch by soaking water through the ashes of burned seaweed to extract soda, then roasted limestone or chalk to make caustic soda. Boil with animal fat or plant oil to make soap.

Knife Sharpening:

Fine grain works well for sharpening a knife. River stones are good for sharpening knifes because the small grain helps produce a uniform edge, if you can find it, sandstone is also good for sharpening a knife in the bush.

Two rocks is a superb answer for polishing a knife, taking spherical rocks, and placing them collectively to make a V run. You may also run your knife back and forth in the space in between the rocks to sharpen the blade a little bit.

Glass-Find a piece of glass with a flat edge, rub the sharp side of the glass over the knife blade at a 30 degree angle until it becomes sharp.

Old school-another knife-Simple rub two knives against each other, stroke along the entire length of the blade with pressure. Stroke each knife at 30 degree angle, first on one side, then on the other side.

Brik or cement-scrape up the blade side to side, maybe won't produce a very sharp edge, but it will get the job done.

Leather belt-you can use your leather belt to strop your knife; it will improve a lot your knife cutting ability.

Home Garbage:

You need to have a serious plan to deal with garbage and how to dispose the garbage.

Cooking:

It's a good idea to build a summer outside kitchen. Cooking outdoors is a bad way to keep a low profile, because of the smell and smoke.

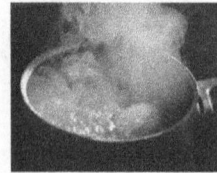

You must keep this in mind and cook with the wind in mind. Don't let the smell of food go wafting from home. That will let everyone know from miles around that you have food. If the water faucet is not working you still need to dish soap to wash your plates.

Items you should immediately hide when SHTF

Gardering

The best idea to grow plants and vegetables is to build a greenhouse or a shade cloth house, it is better to stop the bugs getting in your plants as soon as you can.

Solar Panels

Solar panels will be in high demands; the problem with solar panels is very difficult to hide.

Hand Tools

Basic hands tool will become valuable and a necessity in long-term SHTF scenario.

Pools

Since toilet takes a few gallons of water to flush, you could haul enough water back home so everyone can flush when they go number 2.

Toilets

If you have a septic tank, you can still flush your toilet, even when the taps are dry. Just save water for washing dishes, taking a bath, and refilling the toilet tank.

Toilets take a few gallons of water to flush; you can just have enough water in a back pool in your home so everybody can flush when they go to number 2.

Latrine

If you are going to bug in, you're going to necessitate a permeant solution to the toilet if it stops working. An option is an outhouse.

What is the similarity between a latrine and an outhouse?

Many people use the term Latrine and outhouse interchangeably, but a Latrine is an open trench made for momentary use to receive urine and feces, while an outhouse is a more long-lasting, enclosed toilet facility, also over a hole.

The United States armed forces, and other parts of the world, use the term Latrine to describe the bathroom.

Latrine steps:

Should be at least 100 feet from wells or creeks

About 4 feet deep and about 1 foot wide

After using it, you cover it with dirt

When not in use, put down a wood boar over the hole. To keep insects out.

When the Latrine is full to the one foot line, is completely full. Now should be covered.

Dig a new latrine in another spot.

The simplest basic Latrine:

A large hole in the ground covered by a screen platform for privacy and shelter from the weather.

Outhouse

Is a small, standalone small structure that does not flush. They are used in low rural urban communities to be used as toilet.

Outhouse Steps:

Dig a hole in the ground, the bigger the hole the longer it will take to fill up.

Build a wood frame around the hole, covered by a wood box, or shed around the hole to provide privacy and shelter from the weather.

Cut a hole in the bottom wood for the ground hole, to be used as a floor.

Never build it close to your home, or kitchen camp

How to keep ii from smelling:

Use vinegar if you have some, Lime can also be used to eliminates odor

Make an opening with screen to the outside for ventilation and to keep insects out.

"Anger is only one letter short of danger"
Eleanor Roosevelt

Lesson 13

Skills you need at the End of the World

First Aid:

It is important why people should learn first aid skills. Without doctors, people will want assistance doing CPR, setting broken bones, patching up wounds, and figuring out which medicines and treatments are effective for particular illnesses.

Gunsmithing

People are going to want weapons for hunting and self-protection. It will help if you have knowledge of how to repair guns and how to reload shells. But only assist human beings you absolutely trust.

Teacher

If the schools are closed, it's nonetheless critical that youngsters spend time studying and learning. Remember, those are the youngsters that will grow up and reestablish the world.

Doctor

Medicine is going to be one of the biggest problems in a post-apocalyptic world.

While most people would die of starvation, many would die of a lack of medicine.

Midwife

Everyone knows what the "world's oldest profession" is: as long as babies are being born, there will be a need for midwives. This will be especially true in times when there aren't enough doctors to help.

Survival Skills You Must Know

Lock-picking

This skill is essential; being able to get into abandoned houses, cars, or buildings could be the difference between life and death.

Carpentry

Basic carpentry skills will enable you to fix any structural damage to your home or compound, build an emergency shelter, and do all sorts of other useful things.

Health

One of the worst things is to get sick after an SHTF situation. It is very important to know or learn basic first aid and at least have some books on first aid skills.

Sanitation will decrease, and managing human waste might be a sizeable issue. Urban survival will present many challenges in a city; sanitation will become the largest problem during a SHTF scenario.

Disposal of feminine sanitation

It is necessary to dispose of feminine sanitary products as they contain body fluids.

Your way of discarding may differ depending on where you are and what you have accessible. The best way is to burn them.

After ASHTF, people will have debilitated immune systems, which will raise the odds that an infection will have harmful effects.

Showering day by day could be something from the past. Maybe, if you're lucky, you can take a shower once a week.

Obtaining water and transporting it into the house will be a time-consuming and severe task. Something that people won't want to do regularly.

Cut off your hair; if you are in a warm climate, you could shave all of your air off.

Keep your hands clean as much as you can; people touch their faces many times during the day.

Cleaning your hands Tips:

Before touching your nose, mouth, or eyes

Before and after treating a wound

After caring for someone sick, with diarrhea or vomit

Before preparing food.

After using the toilet

After touching the garbage

Poor sanitation:

Rats will thrive with negative sanitation practices. It will be an extremely difficult situation; rodents will be everywhere.

Age average:

Probably, life expectancy will droop because of a lack of medicine and poor sanitation. Children's mortality will also increase.

People will sleep less:

Danger will be particularly high at night, and you may need protection to sleep lightly. You could be on edge, and you will need to sleep well so that you can continue guarding.

Skin Cancer:

It will be almost impossible to obtain sunscreen. Most people will try to limit their sun exposure.

At first, it won't matter, but as the years go by and people start getting sick, their attitude will change as skin cancer increases.

Avoid infection:

The most important thing you can do after the SHTF is to stay as healthy as you can, trying not to get any infections, wounds, or fractures.

Resuscitation and first aid

Consisting of six steps:

Danger

Response

Airways

Breathing

Compression and defibrillation

These are known as DRSABCD.

Response: Find out if the person is conscious.

Open his airways by placing one hand on his forehead and two fingers of the other hand on his chin.

Tilt the head backward as far as possible while he or she is lying on his or her back. This allows the tongue, which could be obstructed, to give way to the flow of air.

Breathing: observe his cheat movements (rise and fall).

Compression: If there is still no sign of breathing, you should proceed to cardiopulmonary resuscitation, abbreviated to CPR.

Loosen all tightening materials from the neck, waist, and wrist.

This is a combination of chest compression and two deep mouth breaths simultaneously.

People will have worse teeth.

Without proper dentistry or toothpaste, oral hygiene will deteriorate. Over time, people's teeth will decay. Braces will no longer be available to modify crooked teeth.

These recommended remedies are all great ways to alleviate the pain of toothaches.

These natural remedies can help you relieve tooth pain in an emergency after a SHTF with no dentist around.

Toothaches Causes:

Tooth decay

Abscessed tooth

Tooth fracture

Infected gums

Grinding one's teeth

Undelaying health condition

If you have hydrogen peroxide, try using it as a mouthwash.

It will kill bacteria and help reduce irritation. Do not swallow it. If your tooth is infected and you try to extract it yourself, you run the risk of making the infection worse. In a SHTF situation, there is no way out; you have to do it. Baby teeth typically fall out without any assistance.

Children should never use this method, as swallowing hydrogen peroxide can cause major health risks. Hydrogen peroxide may help fight toothaches, reduce plaque, and heal infected gums.

How to use hydrogen peroxide:

Mix half a cup of hydrogen peroxide with half a cup of water.

Gargle the solution

Pass it around your mouth for a few seconds.

Spit the solution out.

Rinse your mouth with clean water.

Clove oil for toothaches:

Clove oil helps with aches and pains; it is antibacterial and analgesic, so it relieves pain effects.

Squeeze a couple of drops of clover oil into a teaspoon.

Using a cotton ball or a swab, apply the solution to the area.

Reapply the solution every two to three hours.

Garlic for toothache:

Garlic is effective for tooth pain because it contains a powerful compound called Allicin. Allicin reduces inflammation, and it also has antiseptic and antimicrobial properties.

How to use it for toothaches:

Start by peeling and finely chopping the garlic with a kitchen knife.

Add a pinch of salt to the garlic and stir until it looks like a fine batter.

Apply this mixture directly to the affected area and allow it to sit for several minutes. It is possible to achieve the same effect by slowly chewing on a clove of garlic.

This method might be difficult because of the level of toothache pain.

Gargling saltwater:

Saltwater is a natural disinfectant. It can help alleviate symptoms by loosening food particles lodged between the teeth, reducing inflammation.

Aloe Vera:

Because of their antibacterial properties, they can help sooth gums, fight cavities, and clean teeth.

Salt:

Mix this mixture until all of the salt has disappeared.
Gargle for 30 seconds to one minute.
You can repeat this method as often as you like.

String and doorknob method:

Secure one side of a portion of the string to a doorknob.
Attach the opposite end of the string through the loose tooth.
Shut the door without slamming it too hard. The tooth is supposed to dislodge right out.

Pliers system:

You grab onto the specific tooth with a pair of sanitized pliers and try to yank it out. You remove the tooth by pulling it directly upward and downward out of the socket. Make sure your hands are clean, dry, and have a good grip on the pliers handles.

The biggest hazard that comes with pulling a tooth out is infection. Make sure that all parts of the tooth are removed. Also, use a continuing rinse and plenty of gauze to limit bleeding and assist blood clotting. Keep the site clear and clean where you are working.

There will be some blood after the extraction. Avoid eating anything that could get stuck in the open hole behind your extraction.

Children's teeth are okay to be pulled out if they are loose.

Eye Glasses:

After a TEOTWAWKI, eye vision will be a huge problem. To start with, blurry vision is a huge disadvantage in survival, from shooting to spotting intruders. Blurry vision will get you killed after TEOTWAWKI.

You must buy as many glasses as you can and keep them in a safe place because they won't be making them anymore.

Neighborhood waste:

If there is no indoor plumbing or waste pickup, the neighborhood is going to stink. Where will individuals place their trash?

Most likely, they will dump their garbage down the street in a corner at night.

The sun, rain, fly, and rodents will vector disease to everyone; it is probable that the neighborhood will get sick.

Burn it:

Folks who live in the country know all about burning trash. A lot of smoke will draw attention to your home. Stay away from burning plastic and burn only a little at a time.

Burying waste:

Items that can't be burned should be buried. Keep in mind not to bury anything close to where you will probably grow food later.

Bury the waste as deep as possible, so animals won't be able to dig it out. Provably, you are going to have to dig about a foot and a half.

Occasional showers:

Showers require water pressure; water pressure won't be available. People will elect to bathe in rivers, lakes, or any location where there's a big stream of water close by. If you are unable to run water through your pipes, you are going to need a bucket and stand in the shower enclosure to bathe.

You will need to warm the water somehow, maybe using the sun to make it warm.

Staying clean will prevent infections and illness. A small fever or cold can become a problem in SHTF circumstances.

Shaving:

Shaving daily will not happen, and sharp, new blades will be hard to find. It will be common for men to have a beard, and women will need to have unshaven legs and armpits.

Medicines effectiveness:

Keep in mind that most medicines preserve most of their effectiveness years after their expiration dates.

The stamped date is the date on which the manufacturer cannot warranty full potency.

Aspiring effective:

Aspirin is safe and effective for years after the expiration date. If you keep it in a dark, dry spot, it will be effective within 5 years.

Nasal spray:

Since it includes preservatives that keep them safe, as time goes by, nasal spray will degrade.

Plants for toilet paper:

Using leaves as toilet paper is a solution for after the SHTF. If you have hundreds of leaves, you can make a great toilet paper substitute.

Lam's Ears grow in similar areas, like arid and rocky ones.

Mullein (Verbascum) is a runner-up to Lamb's Ear because it is soft. Mullein grows along roadsides and in rocky banks.

Plantago is easy to find almost all year long; it is a common plant in lawns, driveways, and wooded areas.

Cabbage or cauliflower leaves (Brassicas) are wide, strong, and hard to break. In difficult times, you can use cabbage leaves as toilet paper.

Borage's young leaves are also a good option.

Yellow Dock (Rumex Crispus) is also a common lawn and shade tree.

Common tamarisk (Thuidium tamariscinum) is an excellent alternative; you can find thick layers of moss in the woods.

Coltsfoot (Tussilago farfara): You will find Coltsfoot in lowland wooded areas that are rocky.

Redbuds Three (Cercis canadensis): the leaves are quite thick and larger than your hand. It was utilized by Native Americans to deal with diarrhea.

No one likes to talk about how they are going to go to the bathroom if the plumbing goes down. But we must work toward a solution.

Portable Toilets

If you can't flush, you can still use the bathroom for comfort and privacy. The best solution is to make a two-bucket toilet, a portable toilet to go to number 1, and at the end of the day, dump the bucket in a low-lying area.

For number 2, use a small bucket and small trash bags as liners.

When you are done, you can tie the bag and throw it away. Having two buckets is a lot less messy and smelly than using a single bucket. Separating urine and feces with a two-bucket restroom system will make it much easier to do away with the waste.

If the water is not running, there is probably no garbage collection. You will have to bury or burn it. Dig a deep hole and bury it anywhere far away from the cooking site and sleeping quarters.

Setting the bucket toilet system

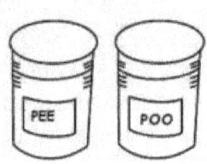

Mark one bucket for pee and the other for poo.

Have a lid for each bucket.

Use a sturdy plastic bag to line the poo bucket.

Close the lid on the bucket every day after each use.

Dump the buckets outside when they are full.

You should have a lid for every bucket toilet. This will keep it from getting stinky and save you from stepping into the poo bucket.

Latrines

If the water is not working after the SHTF, you will need a permanent solution to do numbers 1 and 2. The option is a latrine.

Dig a trench about one foot deep, two feet wide, and four feet long. Stick some posts in the ground so you can balance yourself while doing your business; place a tarp or tent over it so you can have some privacy. When you are done, cover the waste with dirt. If the crisis lasts very long, you will have to dig one every couple of days or weeks. Make sure it is as far from your home as you can.

Wear shoes on the ground close to a latrine because intestinal worms and other kinds of parasites may infect the soil. Also, set up a handwashing station by the latrine to destroy bacteria.

Review:

Dig your latrine into at least 200 feet of water.

Cover the latrine when not in use.

After using the latrine, make sure to cover it with at least one foot of dirt.

Wear shoes every time you use the latrine.

Wash hands after done.

Older family members

One of the biggest factors in disaster preparation is the elderly family member. The elderly are particularly susceptible to disaster conditions. The reality is that if you have an elderly family member, you will need to stay put in a disaster.

If elderly people try to barter after SHTF, they'll expose their stash and be mugged. The elderly will be targets for looting and mugging because of their perceived weakness. Even the use of a firearm by the elderly will be a problem due to recoil, accuracy, etc.

Elderly people with medical conditions won't be able to withstand the elements and the survival tasks that will require physical strength. Make a list of medications and dosing schedules and keep it in an emergency binder. Keep an eye on expiration dates; use the oldest first.

You can't bug out and get stuck in a street and need to leave the vehicle, or push through crows with an elderly family member. Consider getting specialized wheels for their wheelchair so it can go over rubble.

Preppers with disabilities will need a lot of planning and preparation, but it can be done. You will need to make plans before SHTF happens, keeping in mind that you are going to stay put for sure in an SHTF situation.

Lesson 14

Pandemic:

The Spanish Flu infected 500 million people in 1918–1920 and killed 50 million; remember also the HIV pandemic in 1980. Still affect us now. Another virus that cost millions of people was the Black Death, which hit Asia and Europe in the 1300s. The coronavirus pandemic took most people by surprise.

It is vital to learn how to disinfect and treat wounds. When medical aid is not available, you must stop bacteria and disease from spreading.

Rules of first aid:

Unconsciousness should be treated first; the brain with no oxygen can last no more than 5 minutes.

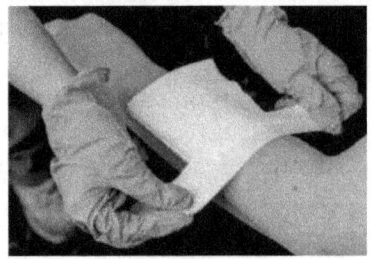

Bleeding is next, and if not taken care of soon, could lead to death.

The third condition is burn and scrape. This is important because burns of any degree can cause infections.

Superglue-wounds:

Superglue can be used to close wounds if you don't have anything else. Some people may be allergic to it, but surviving and staying alive is more important.

Broken bone

It's also known as a fracture; it happens when one of your bones becomes broken into pieces. Could be from an accident or violent drama.

Temporary fixation should be done before moving the casualty, unless life is endangered.

Symptoms:

Severe pain

Tenderness

Swelling

Difficulty moving fingers, arms, or legs

A hand fracture is among the most frequently occurring fractures caused by physical drama, such as:

Direct blow from an object

Heavy impact

Crushing of the hand

Creating a splint:

Pad the injury with bags or cloth. Above and below the injury make a stick with two straight objects-tree branches, a canoe paddle, etc.-and place them in an area across the fracture.

Burns:

Burns are injuries caused by hot, dry, or wet objects. The best way to deal with burns and scalds is to pour cold running water on the injury site to soothe the burning pain.

Then cover up the injury to prevent the burn from sticking to the cloth. Use a bandage to cover it up.

Aloe Vera for burns and scrapes:

How to use it: Break or reduce off one of the spiky, huge leaves and squeeze out the goo from inside. Use the gel to shield the burn, cut, or an area that needed soothing. Aloe is used in many skincare products, and it is safe for most people.

Minor cuts:

Wash the wound with soap and water.

Apply direct pressure to stop the bleeding.

Apply some type of antibacterial ointment.

Apply a dirt-free bandage that will not stick to the wound.

Minor Punctures:

Rinse the puncture for 5 minutes under running water. Then wash with soap.

Look for objects inside the wound. Sometimes you need a tweezer or a scalpel to remove splinters and other objects.

Remember, a bad infection could cause your death.

There will not be any more joint replacements if you crush your knee; you'll have to live the rest of your life with the injury.

You can use a strip-off shirt or pants as a bandage. Do not bind it too tightly. Go back frequently to change the bandage, several times a day.

It is also important that the wound gets fresh air for a couple of minutes every few hours.

Avoid smoking:

Avoid smoking as much as you can.

Duct tape for warts:

How to use it: cut a small piece of duct tape the size of your wart, cover it, and let it set until it falls off.

Soak the wart, and then cover it again. Keep this process going until the wart goes away.

Chili peppers:

It has been used in folk medicine for a long time. Capsaicin is a popular topical inflammatory ingredient for managing pain.

It makes your area get hot before eventually turning numb. Capsaicin creams and ointments are used to battle many types of pain, related to Rheumatoid arthritis as well as joint pain.

How to survive the apocalypse with kids

Kids would be forced to grow up fast, and they would expect to contribute more to the group than we might expect.

Children will be expected to start taking part in things like gardening, feeding the animals, picking eggs, helping with cooking, and keeping watch during the daytime at the age of ten or eleven.

Wild medicinal plants: remember the following when collecting wild plants for food:

If you see plant life growing near homes and buildings or next to roadsides, they have probably been sprayed with pesticides. Wash them thoroughly. Plants growing in contaminated water boil or disinfect them.

Some plants contain extraordinarily risky fungi. To lessen the chance of accidental poisoning, do not eat any fruit that is starting to spoil or showing signs of mildew or fungus.

Some chokecherry plants have high concentrations of deadly cyanide compounds. I have read somewhere that horses have died from eating wilted wild cherry leaves.

Stay away from any weeds and leaves with an almond-like odor, typical of the cyanide compounds.

To avoid potentially poisonous plants, stay away from any wild or unknown plants that have:

Milky or discolored sap.

Beans, bulbs, or seeds inside pods.

Bitter or soapy taste.

Spines, fine hairs, or thorns.

Almond" scent in woody parts and leaves

Grain heads with pink, purplish, or black spurs.

Three- leaved growth pattern.

Some people are more susceptible to gastric distress from plants. Be careful

Seaweeds

This sort of marine algae is placed on or near ocean coastlines. There are also a few freshwater varieties. Seaweed is a treasure trove of iodine, minerals, and vitamin C.

Large portions of seaweed in an unaccustomed belly can produce an excessive laxative effect.

When accumulating seaweed for food, locate dwelling plant life connected to rocks or floating free. Seaweed washed onshore for an extended period of time may be putrefied or decayed.

You can dry currently collected seaweeds for later use.

Preparing seaweed for consumption depends on the sort of seaweed. Boil thick, leathery seaweeds for a short time to make them softer.

Eat them as a vegetable or with different foods. You can eat a few types uncooked after testing for edibility.

Plants are generally poisoned by:

Ingestion- When a person eats part of a toxic plant.

Contact-When a person touches a toxic plant; it causes skin irritation, or dermatitis.

Absorption or inhalation when a person absorbs the poison through the pores or inhales it into the breathing system.

Plant poisoning stages range from slight irritation to death. A popular question asked is, "How toxic is this plant?" It is complicated to say how poisonous plants are.

Some plant life requires touch with a massive quantity of the plant before noticing any detrimental response, while others will purposely die with the best of a small quantity.

Every plant will vary in the quality of toxins it contains due to different growing conditions and mild versions in subspecies.

Every individual has an exceptional degree of resistance to poisonous substances.

Some popular mistaken beliefs about poisonous plants are:

Watch the animals and devour what they eat. Most of the time, this statement is true, but a few animals can devour plants that are toxic to humans.

Boiling the plant in water eliminates several poisons, but not all.

Plants with a pink-red color are toxic. Some scrubs that are red are poisonous, but not all.

The factor is that there may be no one to assist in figuring out poisonous plants.

You must make an attempt to gain as much information about them as possible.

Avoiding poisonous plants:

All mushrooms- Mushroom identity is surely hard and should be precise, even more so than with different plants. Some mushrooms induce death very quickly. Some mushrooms have no known cure.

Two general types of mushroom poisoning are gastrointestinal and indigestion poisoning, which may be extreme and could lead to death very quickly.

Don't eat any plant unless you have absolute recognized it first.

Indications and symptoms of ingestion poisoning can include nausea, throwing up, diarrhea, abdominal cramps, a gradual slowing of the heartbeat, respiration, headaches, visions, dry mouth, unconsciousness, coma, and death.

The following plants can cause ingestion poisoning if eaten:

Castor bean.	Pangi.
Chinaberry.	Physic nut.
Death camas.	Poison and water hemlocks.
Lantana.	Rosary pea.
Manchineel.	Strychnine tree.
Oleander.	

Blackberry leaves

Are helpful for diarrhea, make a potion (like a tea) by pouring near-boiling water over the leaves and letting steep for 5 to 10 minutes. The usual ratio is about 2.5 ounces (seventy-five grams) of fresh leaf or 1 ounce (30 grams) of dried herb to one cup of warm water.

Lavender

To treat insect bites, burns, and skin conditions; to alleviate itching and rashes; and to reduce swelling. Spread the crushed, fresh leaves over the affected area. Lavender isn't to be taken internally by pregnant or nursing women or small children.

Yarrow

As an effective mending herb used topically for injuries, cuts, and scrapes. Crushed leaves and flowers placed on cuts and scratches can prevent bleeding and decrease the risk of infection.

Plantain

The green leaves can be compressed into a paste and spread over poisonous stings and bites with excellent effect.

Though not strong enough to tackle snake bites, plantain can help reduce the effects of the venom of bees, wasps, scorpions, and other pain-inducing creatures.

Dandelion

Is a fashionable liver and gall bladder tonic, and to stimulate digestion, mix one tablespoon of the dried root in a single cup of warm water. 1 to 2 tablespoons of dried leaves may be added.

Echinacea

Native Americans have used it for hundreds of years to treat infections and wounds. Extracts of Echinacea can kill different kinds of bacteria, like Streptococcus.

Scientific research has confirmed that Echinacea products fed at the primary sign of cold symptoms can reduce the symptoms and length of the common cold in adults.

Echinacea contains plant compounds that can assault yeast and different fungi very effectively. Consume the dried root and/or leaf as a tea.

Elderberry

When placed on the skin, elderberry is powerful at treating wounds.

Jewelweed

If you come into contact with poison ivy, oak, or sumac, locate some jewelweed (Capensis), squeeze the juicy, purplish stalk into a slimy paste, and rub it all over the affected skin.

After 2 minutes of contact, rinse off the jewelweed mush with easy water. If you can do this within 30 to 45 minutes of ivy exposure, you may have little to no poison ivy reaction.

Garlic

Studies have found that garlic can be an effective treatment against bacteria, including Salmonella and E. coli. It has also been considered for use against tuberculosis.

Specialists divulge that taking concentrated garlic may cause bleeding. This can be dangerous for individuals taking blood thinners and facing surgery.

Honey

Doctors today have found it helpful to treat chronic wounds, burns, ulcers, and bedsores.

Ginger

Science has demonstrated ginger's ability to fight many strains of bacteria.

Goldenseal

Usually consumed for respiratory and digestive problems. Also, it may be used to combat diarrhea and urinary tract infections.

Clove

The clove water extract may be effective against different kinds of bacteria, like E. coli.

Lesson 15

Apartment-Condominium

Perimeters

In a condominium-apartment building, the perimeters would look very different. The first perimeter is frequently the entrance or alley, which leads to a fire escape. For ground-floor apartments, the outer limits may be the actual sidewalk.

About 60 million Americans live in apartments, and a lot of people who live in apartments are on a tight budget because of budget issues.

So planning for a disaster could cause problems with the budget.

You don't need a lot of money to start getting ready, but you do need to be smart about what you buy to stay safe.

Not everyone has a bug-out place to go after or before a disaster, and leaving your apartment is not always an option for you and your family during or after the SHTF.

Make sure you have an alternative plan in case you need to leave; do not rule out this possibility.

Keep in mind that if you have a large family, disasters get more difficult in an apartment, and the higher your unit is, the more problematic your situation becomes.

Make sure your child stays in the most out-of-the-way room of the house so his or her crying doesn't get attention.

Assess your situation with bugs in your building:

Location of your condo-apartment building

Neighbors you have

Number of family members

Family with disabilities-medical conditions

Pets

You and your family's fitness level

The biggest problem with apartment emergencies is finding enough room to store all those extra supplies. In an apartment, you probably lack space; however, there are numerous conditions you may put together if they ever occur. You are going to have to get creative and learn how to use every inch of space you have.

Start with the basics for sustaining life: food, water, shelter, and self-defense.

Plan on bartering; when you live in an apartment or condominium, you won't be able to stockpile everything you need for a crisis scenario. You need to be clever about what you keep and what is essential, and start stacking those.

Also remember to stock your medicine container with feminine hygiene products; these are essential.

Vertical storage area: stack your possessions like a grocery store, vertically, and create and implement a rotation system so things don't expire and turn out to be useless.

You can use 5-gallon plastic buckets with lids as a dry storage space for supplies. This allowed you to stack them up—four or five buckets up.

Fire is another major enemy in an apartment, beside neighbors. When you live above ground, it is not an easy situation to get out of a fire.

Another concern is your ability to defend your home during a crisis. The problem with living in an apartment is that you are at the mercy of not only those who live in the complex but also those who live outside and might want to get in. It is going to be tough, with far more challenges than those who own a home.

Take a look at your apartment from outside, and think like an outsider: how would you escape? Where would you run or jump? The key to planning a safe escape is the key to staying alive.

If you live on an upper floor, you gain some security; you won't have people coming through the windows.

If you live in an apartment, you'll want to board up points of entry, like doors.

City survival depends on your safety from both the SHTF aftermath and the way people react to it.

Here are a few tips for getting the apartment ready:

Start growing plants inside your apartment. A small container is a great way to supplement your food supply. There are numerous vegetables and plants that only require a small growing area.

A container can be used to grow a variety of fruits, herbs, and vegetables, and they do well in an indoor setting.

Microtrees

You can buy your own miniature orange, lime, and banana trees. They are very small and can easily fit into the corner of a room; they also serve as décor but also produce a small amount of food.

The balconies of apartments are perfect to keep small pots and grow Beets, leafy greens, and spinach—these plants will do okay partially in shady areas. Hanging tomato baskets is an alternative solution; hanging tomatoes could be grown indoors in an apartment situation.

Make sure the pot is at least six inches wide, and keep it in a warm spot that gets at least twelve hours of light a day.

Another idea is to collect enough soil from other sites and, with the help of a family member or a neighbor, cover some space on the roof top of the building to create a bigger garden. You could also build a small shed in a space down in the corner away from the garden to use when the sewer goes.

If you don't have the space, you could try hanging pots from the ceiling or wall. You could also place them on a mounted shelf; shelves are a great way to save space.

Here is a list of some vegetables and fruits you can easily grow on your apartment balcony:

Hanging Tomatoes

Strawberries have shallow roots; it doesn't matter what container is used.

Lemons are perfect indoor plants because they are sensitive to cold or extreme temperatures, so indoor space has beneficial effects on the growth of the fruit.

Carrots can be grown in a small apartment without any problems.

Dwarf mandarin trees are perfect for apartments.

Green beans don't require much space horizontally but require support vertically to grow properly.

Sweet peas take a short time before they are ready for harvest. They grow vertically; provide them with a support like a trellis.

Keep in mind that many vegetables will need to receive light for at least 6 hours per day.

Of course, you will never grow enough food in your apartment to live off, but at least you have some, not only to eat but to barter with.

Collect and stockpile non-perishable food. Find dehydrated foods; they're usually good for 10 to 15 years.

Toilet paper can be flattened to conserve storage space. Detach the cardboard insert from the roll and press the rounded roll flat—it won't affect the paper.

The candles you stockpile must be kept in a bucket. Stockpile waterproof containers, as well as a sufficient supply of cigarette lighters; don't forget lots of fuel.

Get a kerosene lamp and fuel. Buy water storage containers. It is difficult to keep a big container of water because it takes so much space, but a small tank could be the difference between life and death. Change the water regularly and keep it out of the light.

Never be without a water filter. If the power goes out, your water quality may suffer. Also keep water purification tablets and drip filters. Boiling water is a satisfactory way to kill bugs.

Every family member should have a sleeping bag. At night, when it is cold, a sleeping bag can be more effective than blankets, and they are easier to store than blankets.

Make sure to have a toolbox, screwdrivers, hammers, and nails.

Make sure to get extra locks on windows and doors, especially if you live on the bottom floor, to make your home as difficult for unwanted guests to enter as possible.

The emergency lights in the stairwell won't light forever, so you better have a flashlight or a cigar lither to help you have light on your way out. If it is dark and you don't see, keep your hands passing through the wall or railroad.

In a fire, the first option shouldn't be to abandon your shelter, unless the fire is too big and puts your life and other family members' lives at risk. You should try to put out the fire if it is a mall fire. Now, if you can't put it out or if it is a big fire, then you should leave quickly.

Have a fire plan because, in the case of a fire, panic can blind you. Make sure everybody in your family knows about the fire escape plans so you can help each other when needed.

Buy fire blankets and extinguishers; keep more than one in case of an emergency. Consider having a mask for every member of your family to avoid inhaling toxic fumes. Smoke inhalation kills quickly, so it is important to have a gas mask handy. It will give you the extra minutes you may need to survive and escape a fire.

If you live far up, you must have a plan for getting out through the windows. You may live high up, but that doesn't mean you can't have a feasible escape route. Make an escape plan.

A building escape backpack could save you and your family. If you are high up, this can be tricky, but you can overcome that with a good plan done in advance.

There are many outstanding devices to escape from a window building. One of them is the Kidde three-story fire escape ladder with anti-slip rungs.

The SkySaver single rescue backpack is your way out of life-threatening situations caused by fire or terror attacks when the main escape routes are inaccessible.

The skySaver enables you to evacuate from an emergency through a window or balcony. It is designed for everyone, and no special training or skill is required.

There are 3 sizes available, from building up to 7, 15, and 25 stories. Only three steps to save your life

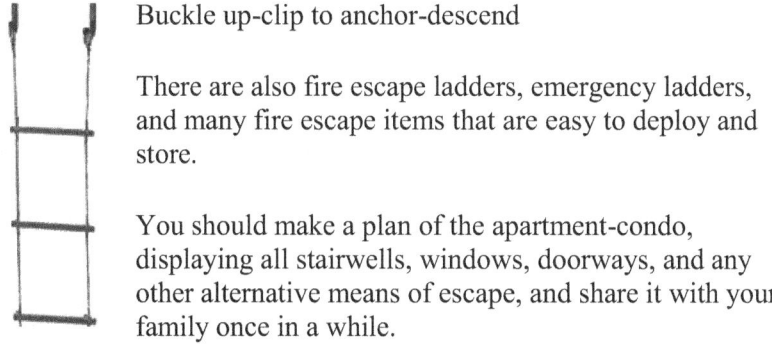

Buckle up-clip to anchor-descend

There are also fire escape ladders, emergency ladders, and many fire escape items that are easy to deploy and store.

You should make a plan of the apartment-condo, displaying all stairwells, windows, doorways, and any other alternative means of escape, and share it with your family once in a while.

Escape routes should be marked in red or orange in the sketch and placed on a wall by the refrigerator to keep them visible.

Remember that smoke rises and also kills; it is better and safer to crawl to the door even if you can tolerate the smoke. Do not open the door until you have checked out to be sure there isn't fire on the other side. Feel the door handle; if it is hot, the fire may be in the hall outside your door.

Be convinced that in the inside stairwell there is no smoke before entering. If it is secure to enter, stroll downward; do not run to prevent you from falling. Hold onto the wall or handrail if it is dark inside the stairwell.

Do not use the elevator; it might stop because of the heat or loss of power.

Can you get away to the roof and find another downstairs stairwell?

Can you escape to the roof, across the roof, and down another stairwell? Can you jump from your roof to the next building's roof if they're very close together? Maybe there is a car ramp that takes you another way out?

Ideas

Toss what you haven't used in a year and donate or sell it. Toss the iron boar; use a table or counter top if you need to iron. I doubt you will need to iron in a SHTF situation.

Shelving: Create extra storage by adding or creating another closed shelf or more shelves in the closets.

Multiple uses (supplies, for example): a coffee table can have storage.

Available space: Take advantage of the space you have and think of ways to maximize it.

There are many places to hide supplies:

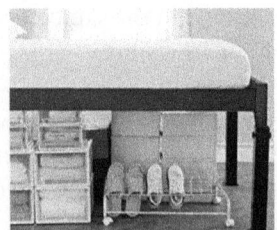

Beds: There are height bed raises, or you can make your own, to make space under your bed and family members' beds to store items. if you need space, under the bed, you can place canned food, water, etc.

You could place under the bed, instead of food, items like seasonal clothes, flashlights, hats, and gloves.

Closet organization: you can place loose items such as food bars, tablets for water purification, and more.

Secret storage spaces-to keep your guns, gold, cash, or silver. You can use a mayonnaise jar, open the back side of a bookshelf, dress a mirror vanity back, or lay plastic boxes one on top of the other and mark the outside with Grandma's items.

Bikes: To save space in an apartment or condominium, try suspending the bike from the roof on a side wall away from the kitchen and bedrooms.

Some people in South and Latin America even raise animals on their apartment balconies.

In Cuba, in the special period (when the Union of Soviet Socialist Republics fell down) and there was nothing, people started raising chickens (for eggs) for battering and also pigs, to eat meat once a year or to exchange pig meat for medicine or other kinds of food. So it can be done if you get ready for an emergency.

Buy food that does not require big storage, such as dried milk, lentils, beans, rice, dried vegetables, canned vegetables, lots of spaghetti, and cans of chili, condensed milk, condensed soups, and powered eggs. Don't forget to store over-the- counter medicines such as aspirin, antibiotic cream, and Alka-Seltzer.

Powered eggs

Try to stock food that doesn't require cooking; this way, your family won't go hungry if you do not have pots and pans or a heating device available.

Keep in mind your pets. Pets also need feeding in an emergency; for that purpose, make sure there is a supply for them too. Dry food lasts longer than wet food and is easier to pack.

A lightweight stove is an essential for an apartment during a SHTF; store a propane canister along with the stove.

Just keep in mind that anything that burns and produces heat will produce fumes that can kill without you even knowing they are there.

Remember, stoves aren't designed for indoor use and will produce carbon monoxide, which is deadly. Always use the stove in a well-ventilated space, preferably on your balcony. Understand the risk of carbon monoxide poisoning.

During an emergency, one of the major causes of death is carbon monoxide poisoning. Apartments are vulnerable to carbon monoxide.

Never use portable flameless chemical heaters indoors.

Never use a generator indoors.

Make sure you vent the gas appliances properly.

Never cover a vent pipe with tape or gum; this will trigger the buildup of CO.

Everybody is at risk for CO poisoning, but babies and the elderly are at high risk, as are people with anemia, asthma, and other breathing problems like heart disease.

Common symptoms are:

Chest pain	Weakness
Confusion	Vomiting
Headaches	Stomach upset

Apartments are filled with lots of people and are usually located in areas with high populations. If you bug in an apartment, it can be difficult to defend.

It is going to be hard to collect rainwater and hard to deal with waste if the sewers back up. If you live in an apartment, say on the third floor, hauling water will be problematic.

I don't want to imagine if you live on the sixth or seventh floor and the elevators are not working how hard it is going to be to haul water up that many floors.

Another idea is to install small solar panels on the balcony. I'm sure they will attract attention, and many people will want to recharge their stuff. Install small ones and place them as far away from the public eye as possible.

Balcony Advantage

If you live on the second floor or higher, your balcony gives you a vantage point to spot attackers and survivors, as well as a decent sniping position. A good binocular will also give you a perfect watchman's spot.

Firearms

The first firearm you need for apartment defense is a handgun. This gun should be kept close to you, and if the crisis is going on, it should be strapped to your hip.

You may need to use it at a moment's notice. Also, plan on storing at least 500 rounds of handgun ammunition for SHTF situations.

The SHTF situation can last months or years.

Next would be a pump-shotgun, 12-20 or 410 gauges. These are among the most effective close-range defensive weapons available.

I'm mentioning the 410 because it could be used by your younger kids, wife, and elderly people, in contrast to the 12 and 20 gauges.

Mossberg Shockwave .410 bore shotgun

A crank flashlight is a must; batteries don't last forever; consider stocking batteries and solar-charging lights; if possible, also a small solar panel and a generator to be placed on your balcony or by an open window.

There are a large number of solar panels you can suspend from a window. Stock plenty of candles and keep them in a bucket; electricity will become scarce or be lost for months or years.

Don't forget water-proof matches and lighters with plenty of fuel; a candle is pointless without a flame.

Keep collapsible water containers; they are a great idea, you can store them easily, and they are reliable and compact. If your apartment has a balcony, poles can be made to allow for a small bucket off the edge of the balcony railing to capture water. You can capture enough rainwater and store the water you capture.

No one likes to think or talk about how or where they are going to go if the bathroom plumbing stops working. Apartments don't have individual sewer and garbage disposal systems, so a composting toilet will come in very handy.

What happens to all of the human waste generated in an apartment?

No running water, no functioning toilet; where does the waste go? Especially on the upper floors?

How long before people are emptying waste buckets right over their balconies or out their windows into the alleys? Or dumping it in the dumpsters and garbage cans?

The simple solution is to make a two-bucket toilet, one for pee and the other for #2.

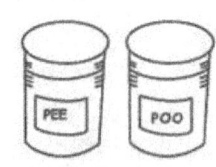

It is a lot less messy and smelly than going to the bathroom on a single toilet.

Drawing here of two buckets. You can't just go all the way down to the garden to take a dump; that is not practical.

You must have a plan for #2. Proper hygiene in a condominium in an emergency may be very important. Stock up on moist wipes and plastic bags, in addition to having an additional bucket, if your lavatory isn't capable of being used.

If your #2 is in a plastic bag, you may take it from your apartment and drop it in an outdoor bin. Better than having to stay inside with the smell. There is going to be poop, urine, trash, and the danger of fire when people want to keep their apartments warm. The disease that follows in dense cities like New York and Boston is going to be catastrophic.

Laundry

Doing laundry is more challenging in an apartment or condominium. A manual washing machine is a good alternative idea; it doesn't require electricity, you can use a big, wide container and a stick to move the cloth around, hang the cloth by the rail balcony to dry. Hard work, but a possible solution.

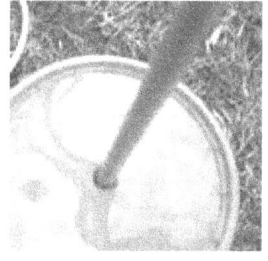

If you've prepared you easily live with your family in an apartment when SHTF hits.

Having a plan for an emergency will beat going outside and running the risk of bumping into gangs, troublemakers, and people trying to survive who will try to take away what you have for your family.

Is it ideal to survive the SHTF in an apartment? No, it is not, but if that's all you have, you have to do your best so you and your family have a chance of surviving.

There is going to be poop, trash, diseases in every corner of the city.

LESSON 16

Must have-Home

In a disaster scenario, you probably would not have running water. You don't want to waste a drop of your stored water. By using paper plates, you won't have to waste water on dishing plates; at least for a while you get ready.

Here is an example of a goal list.

Non-perishable canned food: survival foods for X people, months.

Portable water storage containers (5 gallons)

Purification survival straws and water purification tablets.

Reading glasses: different strength, eyes drop, Sunglasses, hat, Cigars

Liquor, beer, coffee, and coffee pot

Coolers-Cash

Ropes of any kind and length

Home-grow

Seeds, gardening supplies, and soil

Lighting supplies, lantern fuel and propane tanks filled

Flashlights, candles, and matches (the more waterproof, the better).

Communications

Ways to communicate when the grid goes down

Walkie-Talkie, Ham Radio

Coordination Post/Event

Written papers, envelopes, pencils, and pens

Transportation

Cars, bicycles, bike locks, motorcycles, and mopeds ready to roll,

Gasoline in cans for generators, Siphon hose

Health and first aid

First aid kit: mask, goggles, infection treatments, medicine, vitamins, prescription meds.

Analgesic, eye, and tear drops; feminine hygiene products, Ice and heat packs; toothbrushes; tooth paste; and laxatives.

Sanitation and cleanliness

Soap, toilet paper (a lot), paper towels, hand sanitizer, and trash bags.

Clothing

Jackets, sweatshirts, sweaters, changes of clothes, shoes, sandals, boots, sneakers, poor footwear or boots will give your feet problems. Footwear can range from heavy, insulated, and waterproof boots to lightweight boots.

Headgear: Your head protection should include a cap, ski mask, a big canvas hat, and bandanas, which can be tied in different configurations to protect your head and neck, especially for extreme sun exposure.

Pants of any kind, especially those with big cargo pockets, will be ideal for easy movement.

Upper bodies should wear a loose, heavy cotton canvas with long sleeves or a short, light shirt, depending on the weather conditions.

Underwear, briefs, pants, and a bra

Several sturdy belts are needed so you can attach things like a knife, machete, multiple tools, or a firearm to them.

Entertaining

Reading materials, toys, games for kids, Pet toys

Important papers

Insurance papers, passwords, photographs, social security numbers, and passports.

Long-term survival items will be a valuable commodity in the event of a societal collapse. There are many things you don't have, but it would be great if you could stockpile or keep some of the following items:

Even the cheaper toilet paper will be valuable.

Duct tape is a miracle worker in a survival situation.

Baking soda is a multipurpose item that can be used to deodorize, clean, brush your teeth, and bake with.

Feminine hygiene products will be in huge demand. Stock up as much as you can.

Toothbrushes are going to be a big deal when you can't visit a dentist.

Kleenex to help clean your nose when you have a cold and there is no running water.

Socks are critical to keeping your feet warm and dry, plus they prevent blisters.

Shoestrings: you will need them to walk long distances, so laces are very important to have.

Plasticware and paper plates will save you water; you could also burn the plates after a few days.

After a collapse, papers, pens, and crayons will be important because you will need to educate children, and writing is going to be a big deal.

ChapStick will be a necessity because you will be spending a lot of time outdoors. People will be willing to barter other things for ChapStick.

Sandwich bags. It is important to pack lunches, keep matches dry, and store leftover food.

Soap is going to be extremely valuable after a collapse; people will need to clean themselves and their clothes.

People will go crazy looking for trash bags after a disaster.

Not only for trash, you can also use them to make toilets.

Lotion will be a luxury as well as a necessity; after working long hours, this will lead to dry, chapped hands. Cracked skin can be painful and lead to sores that could put you at risk of infection.

Vitamins will be critical for people's health when their diet is poor. Good for trade.

Razors for guys and ladies: razors will be very handy and a necessity; some people will trade anything for them.

Matches and lighters are going to be sought after by everybody. Not everybody knows how to build a fire by rubbing two sticks together.

People will go to any length to obtain sunscreen so that they can work outside more safely. Good to trade.

Zip Ties-You can use them in many different ways: hold a shelter tighter, fix fences, and they are extremely good for exchange.

Painkillers like Tylenol, Aspirin, and Advil will also be sought-after items, which is a big deal for trade.

Bandages will become very necessary after the SHTF for working outdoors, cleaning debris, and fixing windows and doors. Excellent to trade.

Can openers- think about having a food can with no opener? People will trade this for almost anything.

Cheap wine: after fighting and working long hours, a nice glass of wine will be calming. It also makes a great barter item.

Cigarettes will be in extremely high demand following SHFT. Just one pack could be worth a lot of trade supplies.

Condoms because after a SHTF, it is not going to be ideal to have a baby. Excellent for trade.

Fishing line isn't only for fishing; you could use it to make a snare trap, hang up items, and set booby traps around your home, camp, or bunker.

Glow sticks can be used as nightlights, trail markers, and signals.

Plastic sheeting is good to cover windows, repair roof leaks, and more.

We already mentioned alcohol in another part of this book, but it is also important for disinfecting in first aid situations.

Super glue: this stuff can be used for gear or to repair everyday items, even a person wound.

Towels can be used to blackout windows or to seal up drafty doors or windows.

Blankets and sleeping bags: a heavy-duty blanket is essential if you live in a cold city, and a sleeping bag in a long-term SHTF is essential.

Intelligence is the ability to adapt to change.
Stephen Hawking

Stockpile # 1

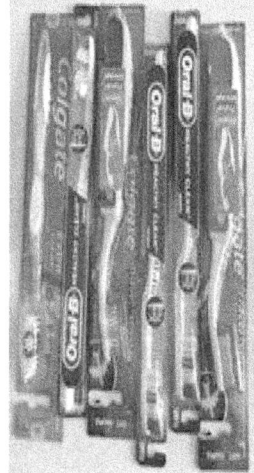

Stockpile #2

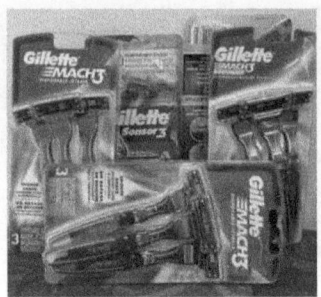 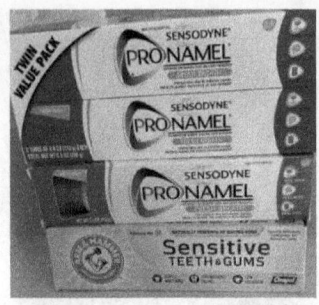

 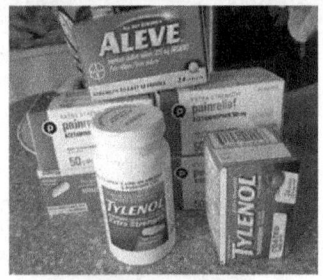

215

Stockpile #3

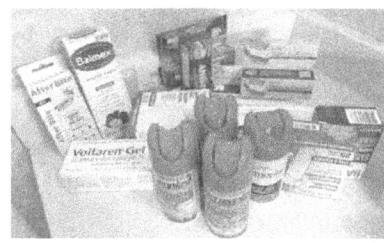

Homemade laundry detergent

Ingredients to make detergent:

Any bar soap

Borax

Washing soda: Arm & Hammer

Shave the bar soap into very small pieces and put them in a bowl.

Add 1 cup of borax.

Assemble 1 cup of washing soda.

Stir thoroughly

You are done!

How to Make a Solar Oven

Cardboard like a pizza box

Knife or scissors

Aluminum foil

Clear tape

Plastic wrap or a zip-lock bag will also work.

Black construction paper

Newspaper

Ruler

Use clean plastic to create a hermetic window for daylight to enter the box. Open and reduce the container lid; tape a double layer of plastic wrap over the outlet you made while you chop the flap lid.

Leave approximately an inch of plastic overlap across the aspects and tape every aspect down securely, sealing out air. You can use a plastic bag; if you do, cut a square large enough to cover the hollow and tape one layer over the aperture.

Line the bottom of the box with the black construction paper; black absorbs heat. You deposit the food on the black surface; right here is where you will cook.

Depending on the size of the box or pizza box, you will determine how much you will spend building your solar oven.

How to open a can without a can opener

You have to remember that the lid of a can is a very thin piece of metal that is made to be opened. For the most part, knives, forks, and spoons are much stronger and wider; use something that is a little stronger to pierce the surface.

Use a spoon.

Rub the brink of the spoon from side to side alongside the edge perimeter of the can, where the can opener might normally puncture it. Rub the metal until it is thin.

Later, when you cut the tab, you will be scraping the broken edges off. Continue scraping until you've eliminated as much of the aluminum as you can.

Use a knife.

The best tool for this task is a good, sharp knife. A serrated knife will make short work of those difficult edges. Grasp the can in your non-dominant hand and use the knife in your dominant hand to make a sequence of shallow cuts all over the top edge of the can.

Continue making shallow cuts until you get it all the way around the can. Turn the can upside down and tap it on the counter a few times to get rid of any lids or rough edges.

Use a rough surface.

When you don't have a spoon, a knife, or a device to assist you. Locate a jagged outer surface and smooth out the top of the can until it breaks the seal.

Wipe the metallic shavings off, detach the top, and get your food.

A 2- little bottle uses:

Rinse completely first, then you can use it to store things like, rice, sugar, coffee. Convenient for food you eat regularly, this not ideal for long term food storage.

Better to store coffee whole beans, after is ground, it starts to age, losing flavor and becoming stale. Remember you won't have an electric coffee grinder.

Bird feeder- Attract birds to your yard, cut bottle in half and fill with birds' food.

Replacement funnel-Cut the bottom off. Remove the cap, there you have it. You can use it for filling other bottle with food or water.

Rain collector- Cut the bottle in half vertically. This will create a wide surface to collect rain water.

Water filter-Get some sand, charcoal and let it sit for some days. Keep in mind that any water filter goes bad as it pores with sediment.

Lesson 17

Backyard homestead animals

Being able to keep small livestock should be part of your survival plan after the SHTF. Relying on hunting, fishing, and scavenging to feed yourself on your own will, in all likelihood, bring about starvation.

Natural resources will be depleted through a lengthy catastrophe; you could be all day hunting and never find any pigeons or squirrels, or maybe have them stolen from you at gunpoint.

Even if you have exceptionally good hunting and survival skills, relying solely on finding food is not a good survival plan.

Keeping small livestock for survival is difficult.

Low-maintenance homestead animals are a key to a self-sufficient farm. This guide is a list of the best small backyard animals to rise in your survival backyard. An important issue is how you are going to feed them and how you are going to keep them.

Choose animals that have simple births, many offspring, and can live on forage.

9 best livestock animals for urban homesteading:

Chicken: Poultry is good for laying many eggs

Rabbits	Pigs
Turkey	Goats
Quail	Pheasant
Duck	Sheep

Birds:

Chickens and geese are necessities. Eggs are nutritious and a good barter item. You will need pens and cages; otherwise, they won't last long. Geese are also a good choice.

Chicken:

Chicken provides a good protein source. You ought to have approximately three to five eggs every week per chicken.

If you want a dozen eggs per week, you should start with at least three good chickens. You have to keep maintaining their coop, or they won't lay in the same place. Also, you must collect eggs daily and keep the coop closed off from predators.

Some people recommend keeping two chickens, but other experts think you should never have fewer than three to meet the social needs of the birds.

To raise chickens, you will need a robust, predator-proof enclosure. This is finished with a mesh high wire to keep snakes, rats, and feral cats out. The cage, in addition, needs to be weatherproof to allow the birds to roost nightly and lay eggs.

The chicken must also have a hay-stuffed box to lay their eggs in. They must have shade and sufficient water, or they will die from solar exposure.

You may also want to keep them close to you to shield them from human beings seeking out a meal.

You will want a rooster for the hens to lay fertile eggs so that you can obtain chicks. You will need a roster and three to five chickens.

Use salt water to check the freshness of eggs.

Eggs should sink in salt water if they're fresh.

Dissolve two tablespoons of salt into two cups of water, and then drop an egg into the solution. If the egg sinks, it's satisfactory to eat. If it floats, it is not a fresh egg.

Basic needs of chickens:

Clean water must be available. Warm water is the major killer of poultry. If it's a warm or hot day, then you must definitely monitor their water and not let it get hot or warm. Hang a cabbage or lettuce in the pen and let them peck at it. They are mostly water, which hydrates the chicken.

Food scratch mix, regular access to grass, and insect control through free-ranging

Protection from weather-rain, cold, and heat. Hot air rises, so it is important to have some openings at the top of the coop. Hose the coop down outside and spray the chickens with a light mist; they won't like it, but if it is very hot, they will.

Protection from predators-cats, foxes, dogs, and birds of prey

Exercise place-to-dust bathing, scratching, and socializing.

A place to lay eggs; a place to build a nest; make nesting boxes with straw, shaded paper, or sawdust.

Somewhere to roost-chicken like to perch at night, so provide rounded branches.

Chickens are flock birds and need company to be happy. Never keep just one chicken.

The best food for chicken:

Choices are corn, grain, berries, apples, and most vegetables. In an emergency, you can feed them cooked rice (not uncooked) and cooked beans. Feed your chicken at regular times each day. They need to eat all day, so always have food in their pens.

A good strategy is to fill them up in the morning and let them out if possible later in the afternoon.

Foods to avoid feeding chicken:

Avocados	Chocolate
Citrus	Dry beans

The chicken can also need pasture to provide food from greens and insects. A portable coop is ideal for moving your cage around the yard so the chickens can pick up ground bugs and seeds. Bugs provide protein, and the ground is a good place to scratch, but chickens can't live on grass alone.

Some people have arranged for the water to be filled straight out of rain barrels, collected from the rain. Less work for them.

Clean the coop daily or at least weekly. Every night, toss away any remaining food and water. At least once a week, clean and dispose of old droppings.

Place the coop facing south, under or close to a shade tree, so in the future it will receive sun in the cold winter. This reduces the quantity of supplemental warmth needed to keep your flock warm during the coldest months.

The rooster is the best-known of the loudest birds. A rooster's morning crow will let people know that you have chickens. If you don't want this to occur, place the rooster in a dark-proofed box every night and let him out during the day a few hours after the sun comes up.

Chickens should roost to sleep; it is good for their health and makes them feel safer to rest on a high perch.

Roost space:

They not only need to have enough room to sleep on the roost, they also need to have room for them to spread their wings and fly to the roost.

Some birds endure heat and humidity more than others. If you live in a cold environment, try to choose birds that are cold-resilient. Chickens can tolerate low temperatures if they are kept in a dry, draft-free coop.

In the summer, chickens need satisfactory ventilation; in the winter, they need to be placed in a closed cage.

How can you tell if a baby chick is male or female?

Males have a less defined stripe across the eyes than females.

Females have darker stripes across their eyes.

How to tell if an older chick is a rooster:

Roosters have elongated, narrow, and pointed feathers on their sides, right in front of the tail. These feathers start showing up around 8–10 weeks.

Can a female chicken lay eggs without a rooster?

Hens don't need a roster in order to laid eggs. Without a rooster, eggs are infertile and won't develop into young chicks. Unless you want eggs for hatching or a 5 a.m. crowing wake-up call, a rooster is not wanted.

What is the minimum size for a chicken coop?

A small coop to keep 2-3 chickens must be at least four square feet. Provide at least two feet of space for each chicken and arrange for a chicken run area.

How can I shield my chickens from strong winds?

Make sure the chicken coop is built with solid, strong materials, as well as chicken wire and predator-proof screens. Choose a sheltered surrounding area and locate the coop in a direction away from strong winds.

Space and coop requirements:

A good idea is to have 4 square feet of space for birds in the coop and 8 square feet of space per bird in the run. More is always better, and remember, your flock will quickly grow.

Poop boards

Place it below the perching area to save time when cleaning the coop.

PVC chicken coop

PVC is inexpensive, durable, and easy to assemble. It is a great alternative to wood for chicken coops. You don't have to cut or nail anything if you get the correct size you need.

Security:

Predators exist in the country and the city, so you need to make sure your chickens are locked up at night in their coops.

Best ground for a chicken coop:

Grass is ideal ground cover for movable chicken coops, also called chicken tractors. Cover the bottom with chicken wire; it is much easier done before than when you are inside the coop.

Concrete is easy to clean and ideal for a permanent coop.

Aside from space, an important issue when building a coop is the door. Think about how you are going to clean it.

You may make a small door to get inside if you have to, but after many hours of cleaning on your knees, you may regret not having built a bigger door. So maintain this concept while constructing one.

How to build a small coop:

Smell and noise-don't place the coop too close to your house.

Draw up your plans.

Know the number of chickens you'll keep. For each bird you have, you are going to want a space of at least four square feet to prevent it from being cramped. Make it a little bigger than the recommended space; this is very important for each chicken.

You're making a home for your chickens, and the principal goal is to make sure they are protected and happy. Begin working at the foundation first, then move up to construct the doors, windows, and roofing last.

Choose the materials

Chicken wire mesh is the correct material to cover the outer part of your coop.

Prop Your Coop Up

Build the coop at least 2–3 feet on top of the ground. By erecting this, you can be assured that their feet will stay dry during the wet season and that they will have a lot of freedom and space to move.

Include a perch area

You will need a nesting area for the hens to safely lay their eggs.

To shield the eggs, keep your nest bins at least four inches deep. Create a space that will allow them to lay as many eggs as possible.

Fresh air

Chickens require fresh air. Make certain there may be enough air through, including a vent or a window. Be aware of the types of climate situations the coops are going to be exposed to.

Use the right kind of material to protect your coop.

Accessibility

Keep in mind that you'll be cleaning and picking up the eggs.

Add entry doors and dropping trays to clean up.

Build a Run:

In addition to the coop, hens require a secure area outside to explore. For further security, you ought to cover the top as well.

Ducks

Ducks are kept domestically because they can't fly away. This means you could also benefit from good meat. Like chickens, raising ducks gives you a lot of eggs and doesn't require a lot of work.

Like chickens, ducks are less vulnerable to the cold. You don't have to take additional steps to keep them warm through the colder months. Ducks are typically immune to illnesses and parasites that chickens get, so you don't need to fear them as much.

Ducks love water, so you will have to build or make a place for them to bathe. It doesn't have to be a huge pond; you can get by with an inflatable or plastic kiddie pool.

Similar to how you would feed chicken, you would feed ducks, and you could also offer them some leafy vegetables.

You should also make a big enclosure to keep your ducks safe; remember, they need grass and room to roam the grass in addition to the water pond.

Quail

People keep quails for their meat and eggs. Quail are easy birds to keep and care for, and since they are considered game birds, they can be kept in some cities where chickens are not allowed.

Quail eggs are eaten and considered a delicacy in numerous parts of the world. You could eat quail eggs, but you would use chicken eggs for frying, scrambling, poaching, and boiling.

About three eggs are equivalent to a single chicken egg.

Quail eggs are healthy but not superior to chicken eggs, but they are a great source of nutrients, vitamins, and antioxidants. Quail are ground birds, and their nests are in the ground amongst grasses and shrubs.

There are approximately five unique breeds of common quail.

The well-liked Coturnix can lay one egg daily between two and eight months. With the possibility of producing 300 eggs a year. The Coturnix quail is an amazing bird because of its fast growth and meat-heavy body.

The Japanese quail is recognized for its ability to lay many eggs. Like the Coturnix, those breeds develop at about 6 weeks of age and begin laying eggs. The Jumbo White Coturnix is excellent due to its ability to lay the largest eggs.

Quail egg shells are thick; you need to use a knife to cut the top of the egg off, and you cannot crack it on top of a countertop.

Most quail hens lay their eggs on the ground in nests made out of grass.

Taste:

Quail eggs taste just like chicken eggs.

Male-female:

After three weeks of age, when they have grown mature feathers, the male showcases a simple chestnut-colored chest, while the female's chest is cream-colored with specks of black.

You don't need a male in order for a female to lay eggs.

Crow:

Both males and females croak. Females are nearly silent; males make a trilling sound, which is not too bad.

Diet:

They get maximum nutrition from their food, which consists of seeds, bugs, cracked corn, and grubs.

Quail cage:

A simple rabbit coop or a chicken coop can be used to keep quails; many people raise chickens and quails together. You can keep them in the same aviary as finches, canaries, and pigeons. Not with lovebirds; they may attack them. Quails need a lot of space to run around.

Quail cages are best with solid floors, covered with sand, wood shavings, or grass, and hay bales to provide cover and hiding places.

You must provide them with a dust bath; the ratio is about 3 to 5 females per male. Males may fight if maintained with other males in a group.

A 13x20-cm cage is large enough for two birds. Wire cages are excellent because they offer good ventilation and are very simple to clean. It is important to have a sturdy roof to prevent birds from escaping.

Quails can tolerate temperatures down to 20 °F.

Rabbits

Rabbits are not as noisy or smelly as goats or fowl. Rabbits are cheap, quiet, easy to handle, excellent for meat production, and breed well. They are famous for their ability to reproduce rapidly. Rabbits can reach sexual maturity at around 3–8 months old.

They don't produce eggs, unlike chickens; rabbits don't lay eggs or generate any products while they are alive.

Rabbits gestate for about 28–30 days and produce an average of 4-6 kits per litter.

Feed your rabbit:

Grass, fresh vegetables, or oat hay; you can also give them dry scraps of bread and crust.

Give your rabbit fresh water every day.

You have to make sure to clean out their pens; otherwise, they will stink if left unattended. Raising rabbits is an efficient way of producing meat for your family without giving up a lot of space.

Hutch:

Your rabbits will have a good time in the hutch; make sure it is comfortable.

Nursing compartment:

Hutches should have four solid walls and a solid wood floor that can support adequate bedding. Hutches should have separate compartments where new mothers can nurse their little ones in peace and quiet.

Rabbits are famous fertile breeders; the likelihood that they conceive after intercourse is quite high.

Choose a proper cage.

The cages should be large enough for your rabbits to stand upright. Lie down and move around freely. Build your rabbits a run; they need daily exercise, and a run will allow them to move without getting lost. If it gets very hot in your backyard, try to find a shade spot for your cage.

Killing rabbits humanely could be very important.

Experts claim that if the rabbit meat tastes sweet like chicken that means the rabbit died peacefully and humanely.

Here is a list of the most humane methods:

Decapitation

Cervical dislocation

Striking the head with a blunt object

Use a pellet gun.

Killing a rabbit isn't easy. I don't enjoy the butchering process, but it is important to your group. I realize that after the SHTF, someone in your group, squad, or family member will have to do it as humanely as possible.

Turkeys:

There are two types of turkey breeds:

Heritage and production- Most backyard people raise heritage turkeys.

Most people raise turkeys for meat. Turkeys are fragile; they are less sensitive to damp conditions, drafts, and temperature changes.

Turkeys will need quality feed, fresh water, living space and a run, clean bedding, roosting poles, and nesting boxes.

Turkeys are larger than chickens. You will need to build a bigger coop with space for the run. They can also fly; you must make a cage at least 4 or 5 feet high. Some people trim the wings feathers to stop them from flying; clipping the wings is a painless procedure. Or top the fence with netting so they can't fly away.

They are not known for their egg production; you don't find turkey eggs in the supermarket or in restaurants. Do you know why?

A chicken might lay around 300 eggs each year; a turkey will lay a third of that, around 100 eggs.

Turkey eggs are absolutely edible; many folks who have yard turkeys declare their eggs taste like chicken eggs.

They are larger, the shell is slightly harder, and the membrane between the shell and egg is slightly denser.

It is better to house turkeys in a moveable pastured pen, like a turkey, or chicken pen.

Tractor:

A shelter must have a roof and a couple of sides to protect from rain, snow, and winds. It can also have some shade in the summer. Turkeys need a bigger shed or small barn. Build a set of roosts about the same height so they won't fight for the top spot.

Water sources:

Turkeys will drink from standing water sources.

Turkey feed:

Mixed grains: oilseeds; corn; soy; wheat; barley; canola

Calculate space:

From 1 to 6 weeks of age, each requires at least 1 square foot of floor space.

Adult breeding birds will require 3 to 5 square feet of floor space each, or a 6x8-foot roost will house around 20 turkeys.

You will need to provide a nest box 18" by 18" for your brooding hens.

If you are planning to keep them inside, you will need to make a dust bath. Turkeys also need to dust bathe like chickens. It will be better to allow your turkeys to free range; they will find everything they eat on pasture, including grass and bugs. Of course, this will not be possible for most people raising turkeys after the SHTF.

Don't keep chickens with turkeys because chicken manure carries blackhead disease and can infect your turkeys.

Pheasants:

Pheasants are more difficult to breed than most birds.

People raise pheasants because they are a great food source. They have a lean, white meat similar to chicken. Hen pheasants lay one egg each day; in captivity, the lifespan is about 11 years, and in the wild, about 3 years.

You should keep one male in the aviary. Males are known as cocks, with harems of hens as many as a dozen. Pheasants are ground nesters; you don't need nesting boxes.

Diet:

Acorns, pine seeds, wild berries, grains, waste corn, wheat, barley, and oats

Weather:

These birds can do really well in tough winters; they could stand temperatures between 40°F and 104 degrees. If a cover for the cage is available use it.

Eggs:

The Lady Amherst's, Golden, and Silver are the easiest to breed and can lay eggs in the breeding season. The eggs are very tasty and healthy. Provides protein, amino acids, and vitamins.

The average cock weighs about 3 pounds, including bones, wings, and legs. Breasts weigh between four and five ounces.

Diet:

Acorns, pine seed berries, waste corn, oats, buckwheat, and sunflowers

Enclosure/cage:

A pheasant pen should be 25-foot square, it will handle 125 chicks. They should always be kept in an aviary with a roof; if not, they will fly away. These birds are high-quality flyers.

You can plant corn or milo in a pheasant pen.

Noisy:

The male pheasant is quite vociferous throughout the entire year, particularly during sunrise, emitting a sound akin to the crowing of a domestic rooster. Pheasants are exceedingly clamorous as well, with their vocalizations audible throughout the day.

You should keep in mind the noise after the SHTF; you don't want to draw attention to your home.

Pigs:

Pigs are truly one of the best animals for self-sufficiency. The quality of the meat and fat is exceptional. Pigs are excellent for homesteaders as they contribute lots of meat.

If you are planning on keeping pigs enclosed, make sure the pen is sturdy; they are intelligent and adept escape artists.

Pigs require a fair amount of space; if they will be in confinement, you will need to have a strategy and a way to manage and process their waste.

You will have to build a study pen where they can stay and be protected from the elements. The pen should be able to withstand the chewing and burrowing; pigs are known to dig under the fence to escape. So build a strong enclosure.

Pigs can't sweat, so they'll need a place with a lot of mud to roll in and cool down. They also need water and some grass.

Allow around 43 square feet for an adult pig to roam around with ease.

What's great about pigs is that they basically eat anything; you can feed them leftovers or vegetable peels, and they'll be ok.

They should be vaccinated to be safe, which is probably impossible after the SHTF because they get diseases like foot-and-mouth disease, swine fever, and E. coli diarrhea.

Goats

You will need a fair amount of space to raise animals that are on the larger side. The goat is one of the main animals raised in the developing world.

A full-sized goat can produce over two gallons milk a day. Goat meat is classified as red meat.

A cup of goat milk has:

Calories-170

Protein-9 grams

Fat-10 grams

Carbohydrates-11 grams

Sugar-11 grams

Colesterol-25 milligrams

A domestic goat will sleep for about 5 hours a night and some will take short naps during the day. During warm weather, rain may cause no discomfort. It is recommended that you have a minimum of two goats on your premises.

Also, your shed will need about a 4 x 6 space for each, or about 20 square feet, if they are going to be spending long periods of time in their pens.

A tall fence is needed-about 5 to 6 feet high is satisfactory to prevent the goat from attempting to jump over it.

Food:

Goats eat anything: weeds, bark, and grass.
They are a low-maintenance farm animal.

Because of their size and weight, they are also easier to handle than cows. A goat gives you the same products cows do, like meat and dairy. Goats don't need as much grass or pasture as cows. When the situation gets tough, they can subsist on weeds and still be fine.

Sheep

Sheep are raised for their meat (lamb) and milk. The exclusive way to tell these two animals apart is their coats.

A goat could have white hair throughout their frame, and a sheep could have a thick, generally brown wool coat.

The majority of goats possess horns that point upwards and slightly backwards, while the horns of sheep tend to curl around the sides of their heads. Goats are easier to handle than sheep, sheep require better fencing.

You will need space-about one acre of land for two sheep-but the good news is that your sheep will be able to live happily on grass. They are adaptable and can live in a small field if they must. They will do fine in the rain.

You will need a small barn or shed for the sheep when the weather is severe. They are sensitive to sounds, can get agitated, and trigger flight and defensive responses.

Goat meat has more calories than lamb; on average, a sheep produces 1/2 gallons of milk twice a day from each ewe. This quantity is much less than that of a goat and plenty less than that of a cow. Sheep milk is likewise made into yogurt. It is not unusual to drink sheep's milk. It is much better to drink goat milk.

In the summer, heat stress can not only impact lamb growth but even prove fatal.

Final Thought

Raising animals for survival is not an easy task. I won't go into the gory details of the slaughter. I personally saw the killing of pigs, chickens, goats, rabbits, and turkeys done back on my farm when I was about six years old. The experience was a violent act and a sight that I will never forget.

I understand that farmers have to do it, and in a SHTF emergency, it has to be done if you need your family to survive. It's not easy to butcher animals if you've never done it.

Don't allow your child to become close to any of the animals you will need to sacrifice later. I know this from personal experience.

Please don't allow your young child to witness the slaughter of any animal at such a young age.

Backyard homestead animals:

Chicken/rooster

Turkey

Duck

Rabbit

Dove

Pheasant

Pigeon

Pig

Lesson 18

Types of edible games in the city

Squirrels don't have much meat, but they are easy to kill or catch. Pellets and BBs can do the work quietly.

Rabbit: You can easily find rabbits in a park near you. They are easy to kill and dress, too. Pellets or A.22 will do the job.

Opossums are not as tasty as other animals; they are nocturnal, and you will have to hunt them at night, which is dangerous in a SHTF situation. Or set up traps. A pellet gun will do.

Raccoons: Larger raccoons have good quantities of meat. Being bitten by an infected animal with rabies can transmit the rabies virus to you.

It can be transmitted to humans if you are exposed to saliva or brain tissue.

Larger traps, or even .22 will do it.

Dove-dove season is a favorite for many hunters. In the city, you could discover doves sitting on energy lines. Use a lure or a pellet gun.

Pigeon-Squab is an unfledged pigeon; they grow up into a bird that loves the city, and they are first-rate for people looking for meat. They are the same size as doves.

At night, you can grab the bird from its roost by hand. Also, the nests have eggs; don't remove all of the eggs; leave a few and mark them.

Some birds will lay more eggs to refill, and when you come back for more.

You are able to tell which the fresh one is, and it will be the one without the mark.

Coyotes are pack animals; they may pose extreme danger if you are out in the woods. Use a .22.

A fox-eating predator is different. Use a .22.

You should never consume any animal that you did not kill yourself. Don't ever eat any animal you find dead; maybe it died of a disease. Handling a dead animal that is rabid may expose you if you have broken skin.

Reptiles and marine life do not carry the rabies virus.

You can eat rats in an emergency, but the idea of eating rats can be daunting at first. According to the International Rice Research Institute of the Philippines, rats are eating in Cambodia, Laos, and parts of the Philippines, Indonesia, Thailand, Ghana, China, and Vietnam.

Rats and mice can be trapped in the traditional way or with a pellet gun; traps are great because they do not cost ammo. Pellets powered by CO_2 are great.

It is important to never eat a rat's brain or organs; bacteria like Salmonella and Leptospira hang around their intestines and kidneys.

Eating Lizards:

Most lizard are eatable, but many have glands the contain toxins. Previously cooking a lizard cut it from shoulder to shoulder and throw away the head and neck, where poisonous glands are located.

Conclusion:

Life-threatening starvation will force you to do specific things.

The Truth-hunting-fishing 239

In the Teotwawki down situation, the majority of the population will lack the basic necessities of food and water, as well as the skills to obtain those things.

The reality is, in an apartment or small house, there is only so much food and supplies we can store up. If you live in the city, do not consider a total way to hunting and fishing. Having in mind to fish and game feed your family after the SHTF situation is most likely a fantasy.

Most individuals' live in suburban or urban environments; most are dependent on the grid for survival. Those living on a farm or small farm are most likely to survive; they have livestock, chickens, rabbits, and gardens.

A time of survival is not the time to look for equipment or supplies. If you prepared before, you would have had time to make your final decision long before the crisis.

The truth is that we get ready before a hurricane strikes. We store enough food, batteries, water, and medications for a few days, cover the windows, and place sandbags around doorways. Get a radio with batteries that operate or solar. We don't wait until after the hurricane passes to get ready.

The same is true here; I'm not suggesting you go out and buy a lot of supplies, but at least you should have canned food, water bottles, over-the-counter medicine, batteries, a flashlight, and other items ready for at least the first month. Rotate your stockpile so it will always be fresh.

Also, you should have planned and have an idea of what you are going to raise—chickens, rabbits? Where are you going to place your cage? Where are you planning to make your backyard garden?

You should have found at least two farms close by that sell your backyard livestock.

What do you think is going to happen after the SHTF? Most people are going on the spur-of-the-moment, and everything is going to be completely depleted.

Having supplies for the first month will give you some time to go the other way from people and get your backyard livestock. Most of us have never needed to fish or hunt to save our lives.

Game animals would be wiped out within the first couple weeks; maybe a few would survive in a very remote part. There will be thousands of animals captured. Rabbits, squirrels, and pigeons will be wiped out shortly after stores are empty.

Hunting will become a dangerous pursuit during the Teotwawi crisis because landowners won't tolerate trespassers on their properties, as they do now.

Hunting on public land will be more dangerous; local groups will claim the best hunting area for themselves.

A lot of people will be killed trying to keep what they own or trying to take what someone else owns.

Hunting would not be around for very long after the SHTF. With no food production, the wild game will go pretty fast, with thousands or millions of people to feed.

Individuals that were alive during the Great Depression tell us you couldn't find a deer, and in the town you couldn't find a rabbit or a bird, and this was a period when some people had gardens and chickens.

Everything will be hunted, including the local park ducks, domestic cows, horses, dogs, cats, and rats.

It will only be a relatively short time before most animals are hunted or scared out of your area.

Another factor will be that with no fuel available, people are going to find it almost impossible to leave the city to go hunting.

Of course, depending on the disaster, there will be different outcomes; it depends on the event, but if a total society collapses, it will be catastrophic.

Many people are going to kill those animals; they won't last long. Everyone would be killing anything that came across.

In a SHTF situation, commercial fishing will go away. Probably all fish will be fished out quickly; it depends where you live and how the fish are taking. Also remember that in a lot of places, the fish were not healthy for consumption.

In the city, freshwater lakes and rivers will be depleted. Unless you can go out in the ocean to fish.

Do you think it will be safe to go out to fish? You won't be alone; do you think you will make it home with your catch? If the other guy did not catch anything and his family is hungry, don't you think he or they will consider mugging you for your catch?

It makes more sense to raise at least one low-maintenance type of animal, such as chickens or rabbits.

After SHTF everything is going to be completely depleted.

Mountain survival

The mountain bugout has always been a special hideout idea for prepping and survival possibilities. Peoples and tribes since timeless times have fled to the mountains because of human threats. Many other books tell you to bug out to the mountain; whether this is well advised or not, this is an idea many individual preppers think is possible.

In a wilderness survival situation, you probably won't survive the night in winter without fire.

I remember spending time in Blue Ridge Mountain; the summers are warm and muggy, the winters are quick and really cold, and it's mostly partly cloudy 12 months out of the year. The temperature varies over the year, from 31° to 85°, and is not often below 17° or above 91°.

Throughout the continental United States, there are particularly enormous parts of the nation covered in mountains. From the Appalachians to the majestic Rockies, mountains are all over the United States. Depending on the geographic region, the weather range can vary wildly. Because of it geological shape, a mountain is a place where the environment, climate, and temperature change rapidly.

Living in the mountains can be hard. Not every wooded area has a stream or lake. At higher altitudes, the air is thinner, which means it has less oxygen, and this makes breathing harder.

With son in the mountain

Altitude sickness can cause headaches, dizziness, upset stomachs, and shortness of breath. Generally, these symptoms are mild, but in serious cases, they can lead to death.

The risk of sprains and strains is constant due to freezing and thawing, and the wind chasing you is highly possible.

Depending on your situation as you climb, you could go from rock to snow, from the tropical climate to winter, from sunny to stormy.

A shortfall may leave you with a concussion, a cracked skull, or a broken bone, with nobody coming to help you.

Avoid at all costs moving at night; the risk you will take is far too high compared to the time you will save. You should also learn how to climb a tree to get away from predators.

Mountainous regions can have a host of wildlife that includes bears, wolves, big cats, and antlered animals. The general rule is that if you come face-to-face with a predator, make loud noises and continue making noises in their presence to scare them.

Usually wolves leave people alone, but on rare occasions, a wolf or a pack of wolves has been known to stalk people.

You should never turn your back on a predator or run, as this can indicate prey status and invoke a serious reaction.

There are five keys to survival on the mountain.

Weather

Air

Shelter

Water

Food

At elevation, a very normal effect is increased urinary quantity. The body's kidneys sense the lower level of oxygen and immediately kick into high gear. And command the body to produce more blood cells to increase the oxygen capacity of the blood.

Also, higher altitudes can place more stress on the heart and blood vessels.

Avoid the edges; make sure that you stay away from rocky edges that are high up.

A walking stick has many benefits; here are a few of them:

Help to keep your balance

Test the depth of snow.

Can be used as a crutch when injured.

Can be used as a weapon.

Can be used as a fishing pole.

The less contact you have with strangers after an SHTF, the better; this will always result in fewer threats and fewer unknowns, making your hiding place job easier.

You must, while moving from place to place, constantly assert your path for safety and efficiency; otherwise, you could waste your time, energy, and effort going back and looking for a better route.

Sleeping in the mountain

Most people sleep better in the mountains because they are tired from the physical exercise. However, the higher you go, the more difficult it becomes to sleep because of breathing difficulties at higher altitudes.

Specific gear is needed if you plan to survive and hunt in the mountains.

A capable rifle

You need a map and a compass; getting lost in the mountains is likely.

Hand-held GMR radio or a high-quality walkie-talkie. Mountains can easily interfere with communication with members of your group.

Some kind of signaling and distress equipment is vital in the mountains.

A sleeping bag, rated for cold, is mandatory in a mountain situation.

Preppers and survival people should avoid mountains and routes so steep that they require the use of proper climbing gear.

A four-season tent can be great, but sooner or later you are going to have to build a better, stronger shelter. It is better to build a remote cabin/shed.

How to survive a lighting storm in the mountain:

Recognize the signs of an approaching storm-cloud cover and light flashes.

Keep the group apart-if somebody get struck, no one will be free to help.

Remove jewelry or metal from your body.

Seek a dry, safe shelter, stay away from trees, go to a lower site and position yourself as low and horizontal as you can.

Place insulator like wood under you.

Make yourself a small target as you can.

You may come across a remote, abandoned cabin, and in a SHTF situation, you could use it for a while until the owners come back and claim it.

Caution:

Rockslides: similar to avalanches, a rockslide happens when rocks in an area become loose and travel downhill.

Falling rocks
Falling ice

If you are going to walk in the snow, crampons are necessary; these devices have spikes on them to help you move up and down. Also an ice axe for traction and pull.

Avalanches are very dangerous in the mountains. There are different kinds of avalanches, but they are all very dangerous. Small children are most at risk with mountain lions; keep them close to your side. Children should never lag behind your group on a mountain.

Rabbits: Look for tracks and set several traps in areas where rabbits may pass.

Where do you hunt deer? Crossing through the mountains in the winter, in the snow. Deer-game animals may be near areas of running water, such as streams or creeks, and also alongside drainage basins (streams and rivers). You are not likely to find many deer at a higher elevation once winter sets in.

Fish: When it comes to flowing water, which may be very little in the mountains in the snow, you could stand over a shallow pool of water with a stick and press any fish you find into the ground. Another way is to arrange large rocks in shallow stream beds so the fish are funneled into fish traps made of sticks or other big rocks.

Insects: Check under stumps, logs, and rocks near banks. If you can't handle insects, this is not for you.

Roots-This may be hard to come by in the snow. It could help you, but very hard to find roots with a snow situation.

"Mountains are not fair or unfair, they are just dangerous."
Reinhold Messne

Everglades-Florida

The Everglades of Florida, the swamplands on the Gulf Coast, consist of 1.5 million acres of sawgrass marshes, mangrove forests, and hardwood hammocks dominated by wetlands. The water in the Everglades is only around 4 to 5 feet deep, and the deepest point is around 9 feet. The Everglades are an exclusive landscape unlike any other on the globe.

Approximately, there are 300 species of fish, 17 species of amphibians, more than 360 species of birds, 40 species of mammals, and 50 distinct kinds of reptiles.

The only place in the world where American alligators and American crocodiles coexist in the wild together. There are 43 different species of mosquitoes in the Everglades. Some are hazardous to humans and animals.

In Florida, the rainy season, typically from May to November, is the most active season for the alligators in the Everglades.

One of the problems bugging out to the Everglades is that Florida averages a fair share of hurricanes. During the summer, the frequent rainy and thunderstorm seasons supply freshwater to the Everglades.

Here is a list of some of the most dangerous animals in Florida:

Alligators	Florida Panther
Crocodile	Wil Boar
Cottonmouth Snakes	Timber Rattlesnake
Black Widows	Florida black bear

Eastern Diamondback: The Eastern Diamondback snake is the largest poisonous snake in Florida and also the most deadly in the United States.

Some snakes that populate the Everglades include the Eastern Diamondback rattlesnake, Cottonmouth, Copperhead, Coral snake, and water Moccasin. The hot weather and abundance of meals make the Everglades a perfect habitat for snakes.

A list of some Everglades animals:

Alligators	Bals eagle
Florida panther	Eastern indigo snake
American crocodile	Florida cottonmouth snakes
Wild Boar	Coral snake
Timber Rattlesnake	Double-crested Cormorant
Black Widows	Little grass frog
Burmese python	Anhinga
Wood stork	Florida softshell turtle
White-tailed deer	March rabbit
Florida black bear	Eastern diamondback

The Burmese python is a nonvenomous snake native to Southeast Asia. And now that Florida's nonnative Burmese pythons have established a breeding population in south Florida,

The average black bear in the Everglades weighs an average of 300 pounds, though they can get up to 500 pounds.

A subspecies of puma, the Florida panther is the only breeding population of puma in the eastern United States.

The safest shelter you can build in the swamp is called a swamp bed. This is a three-based platform that allows you to stay out of the water to avoid alligators or another predator.

If you decide to bug out to the Everglades, one of the things you must avoid, plus many others, is the jungle rot.

This is a fungal infection that results from the constant moisture. You must take off shoes or boots, socks, and wet clothes and allow your skin to dry out every few hours.

Another thing you must keep in mind is that alligators, like bears, can smell the menstruation scent. It is recommended that all menstruating women make sure to cover the scent of their menstruation; the scent will put your entire group at risk.

If a gator bites you, you must punch the snout rather than trying to open a gator's mouth; they are extremely powerful. The tip from experts is to pop them in the snout; the snout is very sensitive, and that might be enough to get them to release you.

Author Everglades picture

Secluded deep in the heart of Florida's Everglades you find the Seminole tribe of Florida. It makes sense that people bugging out to the Everglades in a catastrophe will have to compete for food, plants, and maybe water with the Seminole tribe of Florida.

Less wildlife

Birds, squirrels, deer, and rabbits will all be totally eradicated. Probably snakes too. Many people will be forced to eat rodents. Keep in mind that rats carry diseases.

Survival spear

If, for some reason, you ran out of bullets or you don't want the noise for people to find out your position, A spear was one of the earlier weapons devised by man. Spears are divided into two categories: one designed for thrusting and the other as a ranged weapon.

A spear can be thrown or thrust at an enemy or prey.

The American Indian spear was about 8–10 feet in length. They used to hunt, fish, and combat. It was long enough to allow the Indians to fight at a safe distance from their enemy.

How to make one:

Find a straight branch and make sure it is a foot or two higher than you. The length of the spear should always be taller than you. It should be around 1–1.5 inches in diameter, and shave one of the ends to make a point. Trim any branches to create a ridge to make it easier to handle.

Use a knife to make small and even strokes and cut away from yourself to avoid injuries.

Find a rough surface like a stone or brick to sharpen the spear. Rub against the surface.

Once you carve the spear, hold the sharpened end above the flames until it changes color. Keep in mind that wet wood is soft and dry wood is harder. The fire makes the wood dry, which make the tip sharper.

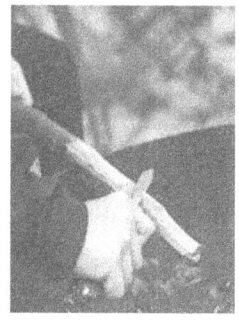

The Desert

What is a desert?

Deserts are frequently described as regions that get much less than 10 inches of common rainfall. An accurate defining factor is aridity. Deserts are about the most inhospitable locations that a person can find himself or herself in. It is extremely hard for humans to survive in the desert; it is also difficult for animals and plants to live there.

The desert is the one place where I lack experience. I have spoken to people who live in the desert and read countless articles and books about surviving in the desert, but I personally have no personal experience in the desert.

Dryness influences other characteristics of the desert. Warm air raises, and cool air sinks. Deserts are windy, and windy situations contribute to evaporation. According to the National Center for Biotechnology's published report concluding that hypothermia is a major and deadly issue in desert climates,

Three of these deserts, the Chihuahuan, the Mojave, and the Sonoran, are called hot deserts" because of their high temperatures during the long summer and their largely subtropical plant life.

The Great Basin desert is called a cold desert because it is generally cooler and its plant life is not subtropical.

Chihuahuan Desert: a small area of southeastern New Mexico and extreme western Texas, extending south into a vast area of Mexico.

Great Basin Desert: three quarters of Nevada, western and southern Utah, the southern third of Idaho, and the southeastern corner of Oregon. Some people also say it includes a small portion of western Colorado and southwestern Wyoming. Bordered on the south by the Mojave and Sonoran deserts.

Mojave Desert: a portion of south Nevada, extreme southwestern Utah, and a portion of eastern California, north of the Sonoran desert.

Sonoran Desert: an arid region in southwestern Arizona and southern California, as well as most of Baja California and the western half of the state of Sonora, Mexico. Other very hot, dry regions include the Colorado and Yuma deserts.

Tips for Desert Survival:

Exposure to the sun during the day and to the cold during the night and dehydration are the biggest dangers. Covering your head and body must be your first priority for desert survival. Keep yourself out of direct sunlight and avoid exerting yourself in the heat of the day to help you conserve water.

Depending on your location, there may be shade cast by small shrubs or cactus, or you will need to seek a place to shelter from the sun, even if it is only for a short period of time. Maybe you can find a rock outcropping.

Do drink water; just don't guzzle it all at the first sign of thirst. Rotation is a better tactic; take small sips throughout the day. Rationing water can become very dangerous. Drink what and when you need it. Soda is not a substitute for water.

Take a good drink when you need it. People have died from dehydration with water in their canteens. Learn to locate water from areas of green vegetation, birds' flights, and animal trails.

Assess your dehydration by the color of your urine; if it is light colored, you are probably ok; if it is dark, you need to drink some water.

Survival approximation time in the desert in the shade with limited water:

Temperature	no water	3 liters	8 liters
122°	2-5 days	3-5 days	4-6 days
86°	5 days	5-5 days	14 days
68°	12 days	12 days	23-25 days

If you come across water in the desert, be cautious before drinking it; it could be contaminated and may not be potable. You will get your body's water through vomit or diarrhea; be careful!

Finding water in the desert:

Dig at the base of cliffs

Try to follow bees; bees are known to fly in a straight line toward water

Flip over desert rocks before night

Soak up drops from desert grasses

Can you drink your own pee?

Despite the warning recommendation not to drink your own pee, you can do it in a critical survival situation as a last effort to survive.

You are risking a possible bacterial infection, but you can also damage your kidneys.

Dehydration: Drinking urine is like drinking seawater due to the high sodium levels, making dehydration worse.

Infection: You are reintroducing bacteria to your body. You are risking an infection in your mouth, stomach, and throat.

Kidney failure: You can damage your kidneys by drinking urine.

Stomach upset: Urine drinking can cause vomiting, diarrhea, and that repugnant feeling about drinking urine.

Heart attack: Urine has an elevated level of potassium, which can cause a heart attack. Excessive levels of potassium are dangerous.

Conclusion: Drinking urine should be your last survival effort until you find a water source.

Stay hungry. The more you eat, the thirstier you will get, so only nibble enough to keep the hunger pain away and your energy up.

If you happen not to have water, it is better not to eat.

Your body can survive much longer without food than it can without water, and you don't want to increase your thirst by eating.

Mark your move: If you ever decide you want to go back to civilization, be sure to mark your direction of travel using sticks, rocks, etc.

When looking for a shelter, keep your energy as low as you can to conserve moisture in your body. Move slowly, trying not to break a sweat. Make sure to keep your mouth closed or cover your mouth with a piece of cloth to help you slow down water loss.

Shelter from the sun is the primary consideration; however, cold, hail, and similar snow can also be an issue.

In many desert locations, once the temperature starts to drop, you start freezing. You better find a shelter or a spot to hunker down before it gets too cold; this is as important as finding a shelter during a hot day.

Have an adequate first aid supply; if anyone requires medicine for diabetics or asthmatics, it will become a problem later on. Bring all you can.

Bugging out to the desert with people who need special care or medicine is not recommended.

Do not sit or lie on the ground, which is 30 degrees hotter than the air temperature. There is also the danger of having a poisonous snake or insect bite you.

Do not remove clothing while trying to stay cool. Wearing garments will help you avoid sunburn.

If you see a dust storm approaching, cover your face to keep the dust out of your lungs.

If you change your mind about bugging out in the desert, look for a road and stay on it. There will probably be some passing traffic.

The top predators in the desert are:

Mountain lions, bobcats, coyotes, and golden eagles. Coyotes travel in packs and make their howls echo, giving the impression that more coyotes are there than they actually are.

Snakes:

The copperheads (Agkistrodon Contortix) are members of the viper family (Viperidae), and they are common snake species in the American Southeast.

Cottonmouth, a cousin to the Copperhead, may also seem like a flash of white, just before you are bitten. At times called the water Moccasin, it is detected in the American Southeast.

The Tiger snake is one of the smaller pit Vipers of the Southeast; however, their tiny fangs can inflict pain and harm.

The Tiger rattlesnake seems to be the second-most toxic American rattlesnake species.

The western Diamondback Rattlesnake, sometimes known as the Texas Diamondback, may additionally be observed in deserts, grasslands, and woodlands of the American Southwest and northern Mexico.

Eastern Coral Snake: Very colorful but very dangerous, the eastern coral snake bears a red, yellow, and black stripe design and venom that is closer to the mamba venom than any rattlesnake.

They are found in the Southeastern U.S.; they resemble the Scarlet Kingsnake, which additionally has stripes of red, yellow, and black.

Timber Rattlesnake: Banded with a camouflage pattern, they're a threat within the eastern woodlands. Found within the eastern United States.

Mojave Rattlesnake: Considered the most venomous native snake in North America. The American Southwest and central Mexico are home to the Mojave rattlesnake.

Safety:

Be cautious on foot in snake terrain and where you position your hands. Almost all venomous snake bites happen below the knee.

Many bites take place when you step on a camouflaged snake, which inspires a retaliatory bite. It also takes place while snakes are startled by motion nearby, such as you walking down a trail.

When you walk, poke the vegetation or shrubs with a walking stick and watch where you step. Also, try to wear boots in snake country.

Be careful with what many people believe-cutting snakebite to suck out poison will probably exacerbate an existing wound.

Sucking the venom from a bite should only be attempted in an absolute emergency.

Bee Stings

Bees are not aggressive but are very sensitive. If it senses danger, it will defend itself and signal its mates for reinforcement.

A bee's sting can be very dangerous, and for people who are allergic to the venom, the sting is potentially fatal.

Home remedies for bee stings

Take the stinger out. The sting may be small and difficult to remove, but the sooner you remove the stinger, the better.

Avoid pinching the stinger; it may inject more venom.

You may need one of these to squeeze the stinger out:

Tweezers

Needle

Pin

Fingernail

Plier

Clean the sting area with water and soap. You can also rub alcohol on it. This will help to ward off infection.

You can also use a credit card, driver's license, or any other stiff piece of card to scrape the skin's surface area to remove the stinger.

Toothpaste: You can use toothpaste to reduce the acid from the venom.

Paste is better than gel because it has the ability to ease the pain of a bee sting.

Another way to manipulate swelling is to raise the extremity where the bee stung you.

Salt: Some of the bacteria in an insect bite will be killed if you apply salt to it. Just enough water to make a paste should be added to the salt. Then apply the paste to the irritated, blood-red bug bite.

You might also moisten the bite and apply dry salt to it.

Tobacco: Tobacco is very beneficial when it comes to bee sting treatment. Just spread it over the affected zone. Press it more than once in approximately five minutes and allow it to relax until the ache is warded off.

Allergies from bee stings can happen mere minutes after the occurrence or a few hours later. Be vigilant!!

The symptoms to watch out for are:

Difficulty breathing

Lightheadedness

Nausea

Dizziness, Vomiting

Breaking out inside and extreme swelling.

Dangerous Insects and Arachnids

Many more people in the United States die every year from bee stings and subsequent anaphylactic shock than from snake bites. A small number of different insects are venomous enough to kill, but frequently the greatest hazard is the transmission of disease.

Scorpion

Habitat: decaying matter under debris, logs, and rocks. Feeds at night. Sometimes hides in boots.

Habitat: worldwide in temperate, arid, and tropical regions.

Scorpions stab using their tails, producing local pain, swelling, possible collapse, and death.

Brown house spiders or brown recluse spiders

Habitat: Below rubble, rocks, and logs, in caverns and obscure places. North America.

Tarantula

Description: Very large, brown, black, reddish, hairy spiders. Large fangs inflict a painful bite.

Habitat: desert areas, tropics

Widow spider

Description: Spiders are dark with light red or orange patterns on the female's abdomen.

Habitat: under logs, rocks, and debris. In shaded places.

Varied species worldwide. Black widows are found in the United States; red widows are found in the Middle East; and brown widows are found in Australia.

Note: Females are the venomous gender. The Red Widow, located in the Middle East, is the only spider documented as being deadly to people.

The best way to prevent a spider or scorpion attack is to be careful in areas like undisturbed piles of rocks or woods, seldom-opened boxes, and old abandoned furniture.

Centipede

Habitat: Under bark and stones by day. Active at night. Worldwide.

Bee

Note: Bees have barbed stingers and die after stinging because their venom sac and internal organs are pulled out during the attack. May be found anywhere.

Wasps and hornets

The stinger permits multiple attacks.

Habitat: It may be found anywhere in various species.

Tick

Habitat: Mainly in forests and grasslands. Also in urban areas and farmlands.

Snakes

Wearing shoes and boots reduces the danger of being bitten by a poisonous snake. Nearly all snakes avoid human contact if possible.

Despite the fact that poisonous serpents employ their venom to obtain sustenance, they also employ it as a means of protecting themselves. Incidents involving humans arise when the snake remains unnoticed or inaudible, when an individual unintentionally treads upon them, or when one approaches them too closely.

Simple rules to reduce accidental snakebite:

Never sleep close to brushes, tall grass, large rocks, or trees.

Don't put your hands into obscure locations, such as rock cracks, heavy brush, or hollow logs, without first checking them out.

Don't walk through heavy brush or tall grass without looking down. Look where you are walking.

First, sever the head of freshly killed snakes because the nervous system may still be active and a dead snake can deliver a bite.

Poisonous Snakes of the Americas

- American copperhead
- Bushmaster
- Coral Snake
- Cottonmouth
- Eastern Diamondback Rattlesnake
- Eyelash Pit Viper
- Fer-de-lance
- Jumping Viper
- Mojave Rattlesnake
- Tropical Rattlesnake
- Western Diamondback Rattlesnake

Lesson 19

Animals' attacks

Red Wolves and Coyotes: What is the deference?

They are distinctive characteristics that distinguish a coyote from a wolf. Together, the red wolf and the coyote are very hard to distinguish. The differences between a red wolf and a coyote are their size, muzzle, and color. The red wolf is bigger than a coyote; the wolf is about doubling the coyote's weight but near the same height as the other. Also, the muzzle is shorter than that of the coyote.

The largest population of wolves is in Alaska. Gray wolf packs are recognized to be in Washington State, Oregon, California, Idaho, Iowa, Montana, Maine, Kentucky, Wyoming, Michigan, South Dakota, Wisconsin, Minnesota, and Alaska.

The red wolf populates coastal prairies, forests, and swamps. Earlier, they were presence from Texas east to Florida, in mountains, lowlands, and swamps.

After an initial encounter, wolves may circle and howl at you from a distance before approaching you. Signs that a wolf is stalking you might include baring teeth, growling, barking, and raising its hackles.

Wolfs work together in packs to capture their prey. Also, the red wolf and the coyote engage in howling to communicate with additional members of their groups.

These animals are shy by nature, and attacks occur during unexpected encounters.

Avoid triggering an attack

Under no circumstances run away; if the wolf notices you running, it perceives you as prey. You cannot outrun a wolf; a wolf can run 31–37 MPH. Wolves hunt prey that is on the run. The best way to fight off wolves is to back away slowly and intimidate them by yelling, throwing sticks or a rock, waving arms, and making you as big as possible.

This is the best way to deter a predatory wolf. If a wolf attacks you, hand strike at the animal with anything you have-a rock, knife, radio, anything. Protect your neck; this is where they bite.

If wolves are lurking around your camp, light a fire to keep them at bay. Wolves are frightened of fire and smoke, which seem dangerous to them.

Coyotes live in every part of the United States, not including Hawaii. Coyotes are native North American that range from Alaska to Florida. Coyotes, unlike their larger relatives, the wolves, live in small family units. Coyotes tend to be out during the night, but may also be on the go in the early morning.

Coyotes' attacks on people are extremely rare. A coyote pack will usually have 3-6 adults and 2–7 puppies. Coyotes have excellent night vision; they can see in the dark since their eyes have many more red receptors than human eyes.

Coyotes have been proven to attack humans and pets and are a possible danger to people, particularly kids.

The standard Florida coyote weighs almost 28 pounds and has a paw track roughly 2 inches long.

Cougars and bobcats: Attacks due to such huge cats are rare; however, they do occur, and fatalities can take place from time to time.

Such an attack can cause deep lacerations, broken bones, crush damage, and even death.

Bobcats are located throughout Florida's deep forest, swamps, and hammock land.

Bears: Black bear are common throughout the Pacific Northwest's forest and mountains. Also they are found in forest throughout Canada, Alaska, the Rocky Mountains, the upper Midwest, parts of the southern U.S. and the Appalachian mountains and down into Mexico, also in swamps. A bear can cause enormous claw-bite wounds that have a devastating impact on your body if the sufferer is fortunate enough to survive.

Remember that bears regularly display predatory behavior in the direction of humans, and they may assault if provided with the possibility to do so.

How to survive a bear attack:

If the bear is immobile, attempt to move slowly to one side. Moving sideways is non-threatening to bears; moving at an angle won't give the bear the impression that you are running away.

Do not run; the bear instinct will be to chase, and bears can run as fast as a racehorse.

Make yourself bigger than you are; make noises; shout; your voice will signal you are not food. If you are holding something to make noise, make noises as you shout.

If it is a black bear, they are like bullies; they often give up if you show them you are willing to fight back. Remember the motto, "If it's black, fight back."

Rodents and other small animals

The Rodentia species contains mice, rats, squirrels, beavers, and many others. They possess very long, sharp teeth, which can generate deep and painful injuries, but that's not the only problem.

They can also transmit diseases, which include rat fever and tularemia.

Foxes and raccoons could carry the rabies virus, and one bite from an infected animal can be deadly to humans.

The rabies virus has a stunning impact and a devastating effect on the human body, and if the contamination isn't noticed in time, there may be no time for recovery, there is any chance of healing.

Bats: I will also have to mention bats, considering that those tiny creatures deliver many diseases, and their bites will frequently expand contamination of all kinds.

Cat bite: The trauma of a cat bite is minor; however, the puncture wound may be quite deep, and it's going to get infected in about 50 percent of all bites. The deep wound will be a lot more complex to clean, and you will also have to worry about the scratches.

In case of a minor animal attack, here is a list of what you need to do:

Check if the skin is broken.

Clean with soap and water.

The bleeding should be controlled; use a sterile dressing; and apply an antiseptic such as iodine to prevent secondary infection.

A wound with lively bleeding must be protected with a dressing or a fabric barrier after applying pressure. If possible, you ought to constantly wear gloves since the animal can carry diseases, and you don't want to get infected.

Dogs

Be alert, listen, and be aware of dogs barking in your surroundings.

Be careful about violating dog territory.

Never approach or touch a dog who is sleeping or eating if you don't know the dog.

Do not run; this will trigger the dog's instinct to chase you.

Speak in calm tones yet firmly to the dog, saying no," and back off slowly.

Don't make eye contact; staring at him may prompt him to attack you. Eye contact can be interpreted as a threat or challenge.

Get something between you and the dog, like an umbrella or garbage lid.

Give the dog something to bite: a branch, a notepad, anything you have.

If you have an object, give it to the dog to bite; if you don't, you may have to sacrifice and take the bite; give the dog your left hand if you are right-handed.

The rules of survival never change, whether you're in a desert or in an arena
Bear Grylls

LESSON 20

Death Body

This topic is not easy to discuss; it is essential to have a plan to appropriately bury families' bodies. Dealing with this problem is inevitability during an SHTF situation; there is no way out of it.

If SHTF, many people will die of starvation, killing, and riots, and there will be many relatives who won't get a normal burial. Most individuals will die in private rooms and on the street without having people bury them.

Some people will die of heat stroke from overexertion, others from illness because there will not be basic medical medicine. Just a simple scratch may get you infected; for this reason, you have to be extremely cautious during a Teotwawki.

Do you have the ability and the space in your backyard to bury the dead? Do you have shovels, bleach, gloves, and body bags to bury a person?

If those who die are relatives, those relatives might take the time to carry out a simple funeral. It will probably be a hole in the backyard or a park nearby.

No caskets, no embalming, no hearse. Only a basic cross and a very simple tombstone. Some human beings will rot, decay, stink, and be left for the vultures.

An epidemic or pandemic presents a whole different challenge. In this circumstance, a body can be very hazardous. You need to exercise some caution when burying or cremating a corpse after a disaster.

When possible, you should allow surviving family members to identify the body and choose whether the corpse is buried or cremated.

How to handle a dead body

It is significant to document the cause of death, even in a SHTF situation. Note the location of the death body's burial. Years later, if the circumstances become more or less normal, you may need to explain the dead in simple terms to the authorities.

Protective gear: you'll need throwaway gloves, a gown, and a mask if possible. You must shield your eyes in case any liquids splash into them.

Make sure to cover any wounds, abrasions, or cuts. These cuts and wounds can be infected if they're splashed with blood or body fluids.

As soon as you can wash your hands with soap and water after removing your clothing, if you have any alcohol, use it to disinfect your hands.

Transporting the body:

Use a wheelbarrow; wrap the body in plastic to prevent the risk of contamination.

The first thing to do is to wear protective gloves if possible. Wrap the body in plastic. Wrapping the body limits the threat of contamination if the person dies from a transmissible disease. Dig the grave between six and nine feet deep and two feet across.

Remember to bury dead bodies in groundwater at least 30 meters from any water to avoid contaminants in the water. The hole should be at least 6 feet below the surface.

Deposit the body in the hole and cover it with rocks to keep animals from digging up the body and scattering body parts. Fill the hole with dirt.

Health risk of handling dead bodies:

Diarrhea is one of the major risks that death poses. Because dead bodies still make fecal material.

Tuberculosis is another disease people should worry about when handling dead bodies.

Bloodborne virus: Additional risk dead bodies pose for people touching the dead are viruses like hepatitis B and C and HIV.

Discard any clothing that came into contact with the dead body.

Burning the dead

The procedure without any equipment will be time-consuming, it requires a lot of wood, and you may need to build a structure where the dead body will be positioned. You can likewise place the dead on a flat surface and cover the body with substances that can make the body burn faster. You can add kerosene or fuel to help burn so the body can be disposable faster.

Burying is also advisable because cremating is difficult. It takes a lot of heat—about 2000 degrees Fahrenheit—to be done completely. Keep in mind that this method will potentially attract attention.

If the death happens in a serious disease outbreak, the body could be washed with a choline solution to reduce the risk of spread. If you have bleach on hand, you could use it.

List of diseases that require you to be extremely careful when handling corpses:

HIV	Meningitis and septicemia
Tuberculosis	Hemorrhagic fevers like Ebola
Digestive tract infections	Hepatitis B and C
Throat infections	Mad cow disease

Book # 2

Section 1-Learning education for future survival

Schooling children's history lesson plans

There is one thing that is often overlooked in books about SHTF: the planning for a new era after the crisis—the education of children and grandchildren.

The world may not be what it used to be, but we still have the obligation to raise the next generation of individuals who will take over when we get old and pass, and they must know the past history.

There are two types of education after SHTF: basic school lessons (reading, math, history, etc.) and essential life skills.

Maybe you don't have any kids, or maybe you have a couple and decided to go alone, or you are going to try to teach three or four kids of residents close by, or maybe you decided to go with your entire neighborhood to survive.

It is not going to be easy; maybe the kids are of different ages and grades. It is going to be a touchy situation; the Teotwawki could last 10, 15, or 40 years.

You won't be around, so we need to teach them all we can so they can build the next generation.

We must have individuals to guard the perimeter, chore in the garden, purify the water, prepare the food, maybe hunt or fish, scavenge, or scout.

Who is available to expend time teaching the children?

This guide provides the person who takes on the responsibility of teaching the children after a crisis with tips for crisis preparation and an almost step-by-step education history based on national standards.

If we don't educate our children, there will not be an opportunity for society to be reestablished, and our children won't have the possibility to go forward.

What will we teach them? We must find out who is available and capable of sitting down and teaching the children.

Teach them reading, writing, reading the clock, the four seasons (spring, summer, fall, and winter), basic general math, including measurement, and the percentages.

Teach your morals, values, and religious beliefs to your children.

We must plan now and keep the books and information you will need just in case there is no school to send them to for many, many years to come.

What if the apocalypse is going to take years? We need someone to take on the role of teacher to teach the next generation.

Maybe a high school student, a retired teacher, a grandmother—someone has to teach children.

Despite the fact that it's a TEOTWAWKI situation, kids still need to learn how to read, write, and do basic math.

Children must be taught core concepts like addition, subtraction, multiplication, measurements, and division. Multiplication tables are essential to teach.

Also other academic basics, such as health and history.

It is imperative to also teach them skills for staying alive, including:

Farming –agriculture
Food-cooking
Communication
Clothing -shelter
How to keep warm
Animal care
Firearms protection
Water collection and how to purify it
Hunting-fishing
Scavenging
When to hide, scape, and fight

Develop a flexible schedule, incorporating learning and schooling time. Schoolwork can be scheduled around the children's chores; more school can be done on cold winter days and less school during planting and harvest seasons.

You could also alternate teaching days: two days a couple of subjects, the other two days another couple of subjects. You could do it only four days a week or even three days if the necessity of time is there.

It will be difficult in the beginning to create order and structure for a home learning environment after a devastating crisis.

Create a designed learning space; follow a daily or weekly schedule; and the person in charge of teaching should create a set of learning goals. Maybe about two hours twice a week for elementary, middle, and high school students.

Teach them gardening planning calculations, when to plant, weeding, harvesting, and testing the soil.

There are many other lessons and examples, like cooking, mechanic skills, building, measuring, and using hand tools. If you can and have any survival books, build a small resource library.

Real, physical books with pages will be worth a lot in a crisis with no electricity, no computer, and no internet.

Some of the best books to look for and keep are those that show people how to perform desired tasks, such as cooking, healing wounds, taking care of broken bones, stopping bleeding, treating tooth pain, gun assembly and cleaning, etc.

One book will always withstand the test of time; this history can and should be passed on to children. There may be a lot of debate; some swear by it, others swear against it—the Bible.

Kids also need some form of entertainment; even after TEOTWAWKI, they need board games, playing cards, and puzzles so they can be distracted, play, and associate with other kids.

History

The discoverer Christopher Columbus, born in 1451 and passing away in 1506, is renowned for his exploration of the New World of the Americas in 1492 aboard the Santa Maria, accompanied by two other vessels, La Pinta and La Nina. Columbus embarked on his journey from Spain in August 1492 and reached the Americas in October of the same year.

Arrival at Plymouth, Massachusetts.

The Mayflower, a historic ship, made its way to the shores of New England on November 11, 1620, following a journey of 66 days. The Pilgrim Fathers, a group of English settlers, were aboard the vessel and went on to establish the Plymouth Colony in present-day Massachusetts.

The Most Influential Documents in American History:

Declaration of Independence (1776)

Constitution of the United States (1787)

Bill of Rights (1791)

The Founding Fathers:

George Washington	Benjamin Franklin
Alexander Hamilton	John Adams
Samuel Adams	James Madison
Thomas Jefferson	John Jay

List of Presidents of the United States

President Term Began- Term Ended

1. George Washington, April 30, 1789, March 4, 1797
2. John Adams, March 4, 1797, March 4, 1801
3. Thomas Jefferson, March 4, 1801; March 4, 1809
4. James Madison March 4, 1809 March 4, 1817
5. James Monroe March 4, 1817 March 4, 1825
6. John Quincy Adams, March 4, 1825, March 4, 1829
7. Andrew Jackson March 4, 1829 March 4, 1837
8. Martin Van Buren March 4, 1837 March 4, 1841
9. William Henry Harrison, March 4, 1841, April 4, 1841
10. John Tyler, April 4, 1841, March 4, 1845
11. James K. Polk March 4, 1845 March 4, 1849
12. Zachary Taylor, March 4, 1849, July 9, 1850
13. Millard Fillmore July 9, 1850, March 4, 1853
14. Franklin Pierce, March 4, 1853, March 4, 1857
15. James Buchanan March 4, 1857 March 4, 1861
16. Abraham Lincoln, March 4, 1861 April 15, 1865
17. Andrew Johnson April 15, 1865 March 4, 1869
18. Ulysses S. Grant March 4, 1869 March 4, 1877
19. Rutherford B. Hayes, March 4, 1877 March 4, 1881
20. James Garfield March 4, 1881 September 19, 1881
21. Chester Arthur, September 19, 1881, March 4, 1885
22. Grover Cleveland March 4, 1885 March 4, 1889
23. Benjamin Harrison, March 4, 1889 March 4, 1893
24. Grover Cleveland March 4, 1893 March 4, 1897
25. William McKinley March 4, 1897, September 14, 1901
26. Theodore Roosevelt, September 14, 1901, March 4, 1909
27. William Howard Taft, March 4, 1909 March 4, 1913
28. Woodrow Wilson March 4, 1913 March 4, 1921
29. Warren G. Harding March 4, 1921, August 2, 1923
30. Calvin Coolidge August 2, 1923, March 4, 1929
31. Herbert Hoover March 4, 1929 March 4, 1933
32. Franklin D. Roosevelt, March 4, 1933, April 12, 1945
33. Harry S. Truman April 12, 1945 January 20, 1953
34. Dwight Eisenhower January 20, 1953 January 20, 1961

35. John F. Kennedy January 20, 1961 November 22, 1963
36. Lyndon B. Johnson November 22, 1963 January 20, 1969
37. Richard Nixon January 20, 1969 August 9, 1974
38. Gerald Ford August 9, 1974 January 20, 1977
39. Jimmy Carter January 20, 1977 January 20, 1981
40. Ronald Reagan January 20, 1981 January 20, 1989
41. George Bush January 20, 1989 January 20, 1993
42. Bill Clinton January 20, 1993 January 20, 2001
43. George W. Bush, January 20, 2001 January 20, 2009
44. Barack Obama January 20, 2009 January 20, 2017
45. Donald Trump January 20, 2017 January 20, 2021
46. Joe Biden will be in office until January 20, 2025.

Abraham Lincoln

On November 6, 1860, in an election that brought the new Republican Party to national power, he was the 16th president. Lincoln was elected president by a strictly northern vote.

John F. Kennedy

The younger president was John F. Kennedy; he was inaugurated at age 43. He was the 35th president of the United States from 1961–1963.

Ronald Wilson Reagan

Born February 6, 1911, in Tampico, Illinois, U.S.; died June 5, 2004, in Los Angeles, California. He became an American politician and actor who served as the 40th president of the United States from 1981 to 1989.

Being a part of the GOP, he formerly held the position of the 33rd governor of California between 1967 and 1975. Additionally, he served as the chief of the Screen Actors Guild from 1947 to 1952 and again from 1959 to 1960.

Recognized for his traditional Republicanism, his passionate opposition to communism, and his attractive demeanor marked by a cheerful amiability and down-to-earth charisma.

He had a first-rate ability as a speaker that earned him the title "The Great Communicator." His strong stance with respect to the Soviet Union is frequently credited with contributing to the downfall of the Communist Russia.

Reagan departed the presidency in 1989 with the American economy with a significant reduction in inflation, the job loss ratio having dropped, and the United States having arrived its then-longest peacetime expansion.

Barack Hussein Obama

A former politician who was elected as the 44th president of the United States from January 20, 2009, to January 20, 2017.

Member of the Democratic Party. He created history when he was elected the first African-American president of the United States. He became the first African-American president of the Harvard Law Review. He served as a U.S. senator from Illinois from 2005 to 2008.

Donald John Trump

An American media personality and businessman, a Republican from New York City. He made history when he became the first president without prior public office or military background. He was elected the 45th president of the United States from January 20, 2017 to January 20, 2021. Donald Trump's slogan was "Make America First". According to the Statista Research Department and the White House, as of January 20, 2023, he has approximately 88.7 million followers on his Twitter accounts, registering the biggest audience across all social media platforms.

Joe Biden

The 46th president, he won the election on November 3. 2020. The oldest person to assume the presidency, a Democrat, was 78 age old on inauguration day. Under his administration, the worst border crisis in American history has been created. Migrant deaths, narcotics seizures, and suspected terrorists illegally crossing the border. According to NBC News, illegal migrants crossing the southern border in 2022 topped 2.76 million.

Section 2

Assassination in the United States

Abraham Lincoln, the sixteenth president of the United States, was executed on April 14, 1865 by stage actor John Wilkes Booth while in attendance at the play Our American Cousin at Ford's Theater in Washington, D.C. He became the first president to be assassinated in the United States.

James A. Garfield the 20th president was shot at 9.30 am in Washington, DC 1881 by Charles J. Guiteau. He died in Elberon, New Jersey 79 days later on September 19, 1881.

William McKinley the 25th president was shot in Buffalo, New York in 1901 by Leon Czolgosz, he died eight days later.

John F. Kennedy, the 32nd president of the United States, was killed on Friday, November 22, 1963, at 12.30 p.m. in Dallas, Texas, while traveling in a presidential procession through Dealey Plaza. He was shot from the nearby Texas School Book Depository by Lee Harvey Oswald.

Oswald was never brought to trial, as during his transfer after being apprehended, he was fatally shot by Jack Ruby, a grief-stricken owner of a nightspot in Dallas.

Malcom X, an African American Muslim minister and human activist, was assassinated in Manhattan, New York, on February 21, 1965.

On April 4, 1968, Martin Luther King, Jr., a clergyman of the Baptist faith and the creator of the Southern Christian Leadership Conference, was murdered in Memphis, Tennessee. Martin Luther King had headed the civil rights organization since the mid-1950s, using a series of speeches and nonviolent march to fight segregation.

I Have a Dream is a published speech given by activist Martin Luther King, Jr. around the Lincoln Memorial during the March on Washington, DC. On August 28, 1963, he called for an end to racism in the United States. King's dream speech would play an important role in passing the 1964 Civil Rights Act.

The speech was a significant moment for the civil rights movement and is one of the most iconic speeches in American history.

President candidate Robert F. Kennedy was mortally wounded by Sirhan Sirhan after midnight at the Ambassador Hotel in Los Angeles on June 5, 1968. Kennedy was a senator from New York and a 1968 democratic presidential candidate. Sirhan was a Palestinian with strong anti-Zionist and pro-Palestinian beliefs.

President Reagan was shot and wounded by John Hinckley, Jr., with a .22 caliber revolver on March 30, 1981, while leaving the Hilton Hotel in Washington, D.C.

Wars

Spanish-American war

On February 15, 1898, a colossal blast from an unidentifiable source submerged the warship USS Maine in Havana Harbor, Cuba, claiming the lives of 260 people. Within a span of three months, the United States emerged victorious war in a resounding manner. U.S forces were fighting on land and sea, and in August the fighting was over.

Most Cubans who lived in that period claimed it was the Americans who sank the Maine as an excuse to invade Cuba, and that the Cubans who had been fighting the Spanish for years claimed the war was almost over.

In 1976, a committee of American naval investigators determined that the Maine explosion was created by a fire that ignited its ammunition supplies, not by Spanish mine or an act of sabotage.

USA Wars

The World War 1 began in 1914. Often abbreviated as WW1, was one of the deadliest global conflicts in history. Dates: July 28, 1914- November 11, 1918

Place: Europe, Africa, Middle East, Pacific Ocean, Pacific Islands

World War II, often abbreviated as WW II," was an international confrontation that continued from 1939–1945.

The main participants were Germany, Italy, Japan, and the Allies: France, Great Britain, the United States, and the Soviet Union.

World War II was the ultimate critical and full-scale war in history, including more than 30 countries and created by the Nazi invasion of Poland.

The assault on Pearl Harbor was a surprise military attack by the Imperial Japanese Navy against the United States naval base at Pearl Harbor in Honolulu, Hawaii, on Sunday, December 7, 1941, at 8 a.m.

On August 6, 1945, throughout World War II, an American B-29 bomber dropped the primary deployed atomic bomb over the Japanese city of Hiroshima, killing right away an estimated 80,000 people and probably thousands more later of radiation exposure.

Three days later, a second B29 dropped another A-bomb on Nagasaki, killing a probable 40, 000 more people. Japan's Emperor Hirohito broadcast his country's total surrender on radio on August 15, mentioning the devastating power of a new and most brutal bomb.

The Korean War, which lasted from 1950 to 1953, was fought between North and South Korea following five years of hostilities. When North Korea attacked South Korea on June 25, 1950, the war officially started. On June 27, 1950, the United States joined the Korean War. The Korean War was a conflict that occurred after World War II.

The Vietnam War pitted the North against South Vietnam and the United States. By 1969, more than 500,000 U.S. military personnel were stationed in Vietnam. The war ended when U.S. forces withdrew in 1973, and Vietnam unified under communist control two years later. America paid a terrible price in the Vietnam War. An estimated 58,220 U.S. soldiers died as a result of the war, over 150,000 were wounded, and some 1,600 were missing.

The Gulf War, from August 1990 to February 1991, was a war waged by coalition forces from 35 nations led by the United States against Iraq in response to Iraq's invasion of Kuwait.

Operation Desert was a series of efforts that occurred after the Gulf War had actually ended. Operation Desert Storm came about from January 17 to February 28 of the same year.

The Unite States launched the war in Afghanistan after September 11, 2001 terrorist attacks. Thousands die, with a $2 trillion price tag. President Joe Biden withdraws from Afghanistan in a disgraceful, shameful way according to experts in the field. Leaving behind American personal and contributors to American soldiers.

American Generals

George Smith Patton Jr. (November 11, 1885–December 21, 1945) was a general of the United States Army who commanded the U.S. Seventh Army in the Mediterranean in World War II for the U.S. Following the Allied invasion of Normandy in June 1944, the Third Army arrived in France and Germany. A fantastic, incredible, controversial, larger-than-life person

Douglas MacArthur (1880–1964) was an American general who supervise the Southwest Pacific in World War II (1939–1945), directed the Allied occupation of postwar Japan, and led United States Nations forces in the Korean War (1950–1953). A larger-than-life figure.

Dwight David Eisenhower was an American military officer who served as the 34th president of the United States from 1953–1961. During World War II, he acted as Supreme Commander of the Allied Expeditionary Force in Europe and attained the five-star rank of General of the Army.

History in time

Adolf Hitler (April 1989–April 30, 1945) was a German politician and the leader of Nazi Germany. He became Chancellor of Germany in 1933 after a democratic election in 1932. He became the Führer (leader) of Nazi Germany in 1934.

The Holocaust was a mass execution in which Nazi Germany methodically killed people during World War II. About six million Jews were killed. Concentration camps and gas chambers were used in German extermination camps.

The Allied invasion of Normandy in Operation Overlord on Tuesday, June 6, 1944, included landing operations and related airborne operations. This was known as the Normandy landing. Commonly known as D-Day and known by the codename Operation Neptune. The scale of the seaborne invasion was unprecedented in history.

Young soldiers from the United States, the UK, and Canada stormed the seashores of Normandy, France, in a bold strategy to push the Nazis out of Western Europe and turn the tide.

According to approximations, more than 4,000 Allied troops lost their lives during the D-Day invasion, with thousands more wounded or missing.

The fall of the Berlin Wall in November 1889

The Soviet Union dissolved in December 1991.

Osama bin Laden, the mastermind behind the September 11, 2001, terrorist attack in the United States, was killed by U.S. forces on May 2, 2011 during a raid on his compound hideout in Pakistan.

On January 3, 2020, the U.S. killed Qasem Soleimani, an Iranian major general, using a drone at a Bagdad airport. Soleimani, head of the Islamic Revolutionary Guards Corps, became the architect of Tehran's conflicts in the Middle East.

President Trump relocated the embassy from Tel Aviv to Jerusalem. The embassy inaugurated its Jerusalem site on May 14, 2018. Many other presidents talked about doing this for years, but it never happened.

Decision for Disaster Bay of Pig-1961

John F. Kennedy canceled a second planned air strike that might have completed the job.

The Cuban exile fighter force felt betrayed by the United States under the John F. Kennedy government, which left them without bullets, any supplies like water or food, or a back-up battle on the ground like they were promised before they landed in Cuba.

Some expeditionary forces claim that some young Cuban exile fighters die escaping the invasion of thirst in the ocean in small craft, with the American destroyer standing afraid to help them in front of them because John Kennedy backs out of the situation.

After the Bay of Pigs, Cuba was supported by the Soviet Union, so any attacks in Cuba may invited a response from the Soviets.

This is also why they didn't help the invasion: because Kennedy was scared off a Russian attack during the Cuban Missile Crisis in 1962, they were also afraid of a Russian attack on Berlin or any other Western city or country.

Many experts think that John Kennedy and his brother were assassinated because the top military power people in the U.S.A. were disappointed in the way the United States looked around the world for this fiasco. Also remember that Robert Kennedy persecuted some Mafia members that supposedly helped John become president.

Also, what about the Cuban freedom fighters who died because John Kennedy left them alone because of his cowardice? What about those who die of thirst in the ocean with the American destroyer looking at them? So many people felt betrayed by the Kennedys.

Don't forget Fidel Castro; according to him, the Kennedys brother attempted to take his life on various occasions. Castro once said to the Kennedys, "What you are trying to do to me, I can do it to you too".

Take a closer look at the world's communist head of state.

Vladimir Ilych Ulyanow, 22 April, 1870–21 January 1924 better well-known as Lenin, was a Russian revolutionary, lawyer, politician, and political theorist. He served in the Soviet Union's administration from 1922 to 1924 as well as in Soviet Russia from 1917 to 1924. Lenin passed away on January 21, 1924.

The Soviet Union was governed by Joseph Stalin from 1924 until his death in 1953. He consolidated power to become a dictator by 1928, instituting a reign of death and terror. Some historians estimate that the number of deaths brought on by Stalin's rule is about 20 million or more.

Mao Zedong, December 26, 1893–September 9, 1976 was a Chinese communist revolutionary who became the founding father of the People's Republic of China. From 1949 to 1996, his policy led to the deaths of up to 45 million people. Not only were people subjected to murder during communism, but also to repression, violations of their rights to free speech and religion, and loss of their property rights.

More people were killed by communist states than by all other repressive regimes combined—up to 100 million.

Fidel Castro Ruiz (August 13, 1926–November 25, 2016) was a Cuban revolutionary and politician who was the Cuban leader from 1958 to 2008. Ideologically a Marxist-Lenin nationalist, Castro, affiliated with the Soviet Union, permitted the Soviets to position nuclear weapons in Cuba, creating the Cuban Missile Crisis in 1962. The longest-serving head of state within the twentieth and twenty-first centuries, Castro closed opposition newspapers, jailed thousands of political opponents, and suspended free elections.

Dictator who oversaw human rights abuses, killed hundreds of people in the firing squat, caused the exodus of more than a million Cubans, and impoverished the county's economy.

The Castro Archives estimate that more than 11,000 people were executed in Cuba between 1959 and 2016. During the Cuban exodus, millions of Cubans from diverse societies emigrated.

The Kim family dynasty is a three-generation lineage of North Korean leadership. North Korea is officially the Democratic People's Republic of Korea. Kim Il-sung was the first leader of North Korea. When he passed, the supreme leader was passed to his son Kim-Jon-Il and then to his grandson Kim-Jong-un. North Korea's supreme leader, Kim Jong-un, is a one-party socialist state with a cult of personality around the Kim family.

It is unlawful for North Koreans to leave the country without government permission. Phones are only installed for senior government officials.

The Chinese Communist Party is the founding and ruling party of modern China. The party has maintained its political monopoly since Mao Zedong founded it in 1949. Chinese leader Xi has had complete control over the party since coming to power in 2012.

Military minorities' repression, state control over private companies, and other actions like human rights violations. Leninist system states remain, like those of the modern Chinese, Cuba, North Korea, and Laos.

Tiananmen Square was a student-led protest that took place in Beijing's Tiananmen Square in 1989. In the incident known as the Tiananmen Massacre, soldiers using tanks and assault rifles opened fire on the protesters before they were violently put down.

The number of fatalities and injured people is estimated to range from a few thousand to thousands.

The biggest targets for Marxism system have always been the family, religion, and civil society institutions.

American Astronauts

Alan Shepard became the first American man to travel in space on May 5, 1961, in a 15-minute suborbital fight aboard NASA Mercury Space Freedom **7**.

John Glean was the first American astronaut to orbit the earth three times on February 20, 1962. Soviet cosmonaut Yuri Gagarin completed one orbit of the earth on April 12, 1961.

Apollo 11, the first humans ever to land on the moon were the American astronauts Neil Armstrong and Edwin "Buzz" Aldrin on July 20, 1969, on a Module Eagle. Michael Collins flew the command module Columbia in lunar orbit, while Buzz and Nail were in the moon. Six hours later, Armstrong became the first person to walk on the moon, and moments later, Aldrin became the second man to walk on the moon. Millions of people watch it live as it happens on TV.

Apollo 13 (April 11–17, 1970) was the seventh crewed mission in the Apollo space program and the third meant to touch down on the moon. The lunar touchdown was aborted after an oxygen tank fails.

The crew alternatively looped around the moon and safely returned to Earth on April 17. The mission was commanded by James A. Lovell, Fred W. Haise and Jack Swigert in the Commander module.

Aldrin moon foot print

John L. Swigert became a substitute for Ken Mattingly, who became grounded after exposure to Rubella. A tale of survival and victory in space. The people from earth stood still, everybody praying and hoping the trip back from the moon was a possible success; if they had missed the Earth, they would have died a lonely death in space when their oxygen ran out. And the entry to earth just happens like a miracle.

Section 3 Basic

Computer World

The most commonly cited name when referring to who invented the first computer is Charles Babbage. Babbage (1791–1871) was a British polymath.

On April 4, 1975, at an era when most Americans operated typewriters, early years buddies Bill Gates and Paul Allen created Microsoft, a commercial enterprise that makes computer software.

1976: On April fool's Day, Steve Jobs and Steve Wozniak co-found Apple Computer. They reveal the Apple I, the first PC with a single-circuit board and ROM.

1977: Radio Shack began its initial production run of 3,000 TRS-80 Brand 1 computers, critically known as the "Trash 80."

1977: The first West Coast Computer Fair is organized in San Francisco.

Jobs and Wozniak exhibit the Apple II computer at the fair.

1979: VisiCalc, the primary computerized spreadsheet application, is presented.

1979: MicroPro International, founded by software engineer Seymour Rubenstein, announces WordStar, the world's first commercially efficient word processor.

1981: "Acorn," IBM's first personal computer, is launched onto the market. Other characteristics include a display, printer, two diskette drives, extra memory, a game adapter, and more.

1983: The Apple Lisa, standing for Integrated Software Architecture, is also the name of Steve Jobs' daughter.

1984: The Apple Macintosh is publicized to the world in the course of a Superbowl commercial.

1985: Microsoft releases Windows in November 1985.

1996: Sergey Brin and Larry Page build the Google search engine at Stanford University.

1997: Wi-Fi, the abbreviated expression for "wireless fidelity," is introduced.

2001: Mac OS X is launched through Apple, replacing its general Mac Operating System.

2006: The MacBook Pro from Apple gets into stores.

2009: Microsoft presents Windows 7 on July 22.

2010: The iPad, Apple's excellent hand-held tablet, is revealed.

2011: Google publicizes the Chromebook, which runs on Google Chrome OS.

2015: Apple reveals the Apple Watch. Microsoft releases Windows 10.

On April 30, 1993, it was announced that the World Wide Web was for everybody.

Section 4

Music revolution

Elvis Presley, the King of Rock and Roll, was the only man to be known in the four corners of the earth by his first name—Elvis.

The first live satellite broadcast, Aloha from Hawaii, was the first live satellite TV broadcast to broadcast a single performer.

The production cost was a total of $4 million dollars, equivalent to $15.26 million dollars in 2021, a record at the time of its broadcast.

More than 1 billion people watched Elvis' "Aloha from Hawaii" via satellite on January 14, 1973. Elvis Presley died on August 16, 1977, in the bathroom at his Graceland estate in Memphis, Tennessee, at age 42.

On February 7, 1964, the Beatles arrived at John F. Kennedy Airport, greeted by thousands of fans, to play their first concert in America.

On the evening of December 8, 1980, John Lennon, one of the Beatles, was shot to death in the archway of the Dakota, his home in New York City. The killer was an American Beatle fan who was jealous of Lennon's wealthy lifestyle, alongside his 1966 remark that the Beatles "were more popular than Jesus".

Major Pop Star

Frank Sinatra was the first and most important pop star. In 1944, the Sinatra craze reached an all-time high.

1955: James Dean- Dean was the symbolic teen idol; in fact, he was the first of his kind. Every actor that came after him tried to imitate him. He was thought of as a rebel. He was killed in a two-car crash near Paso Robles, CA, on September 30, 1955, at just 24 years old.

1956: Elvis Presley, known as the king," changed the landscape of teenage fandom forever, shaking his hips on stage that made girls go nuts. Parents did not like him; some even said he was the devil.

1957: Pat Boone was the second-bestselling performer of the whole era.

1957: Canadian singer and song writer Paul Anka, at 16 years old, became a teen heartthrob idol; his hit Diana sold more than 20 million copies, and he wrote song hits for many famous singers. Among his hits are Lonely Boy, Put Your Head on My Shoulders; he also wrote the words to My Way" for Sinatra; Elvis sang that song; and the Tonight Show theme with Johnny Carson.

1957: Neil Sedaka, an American singer, writer, and pianist. In 1957, Neil sold millions of records internationally and has written or co-written over 500 songs for himself and other singers. His hits, among others, are "Oh! Carol, Calendar Girl, Little Devil, Happy Birthday Sweet Sixteen, and "Breaking Up is hard to Do.

1958: Ricky Nelson's album hit number one in 1958 with "Poor Little Fool" and in 1961 with Traveling Man." On New Year's Eve, he was a passenger on a plane that crashed while trying to make an emergency landing at 5.14 p.m. in a field outside De Kalb, Texas. The pilots survived; all seven passengers died.

1959 Franky Avalon released four top 10 songs in 1959: Venus, Why, Just Ask your heart, and Bobby Sox to Stockings. He was only 19 at the time. Years later, he played the Teen Angel singing in the movie Grease: Beauty School Dropout.

1960: Annette Funicello was the first important female teen idol. She played in the movie Beach Party alongside teen idol Franky Avalon. She was on the Mickey Mouse Club and received thousands of letters a month; she also appeared in Disney series like Zorro and The Magical World of Disney. Her most notable singles are O Dios Mio, First Name Initial, Tall Paul, and Pineapple Princess."

1961- 1971 The Beach Boys are an American rock band; they were a purely pop group. Their Californian tune was adored by teenagers. Hits include Baby Blue, The Lonely Sea, Little Honda, Be True to Your School, Help Me, Rhonda, Summer's Gone, Surfing U.S.A. and many others.

Cher American singer rose to fame in 1965 duo with husband Sonny, often referred by the media as the Goodness of pop.

Later launched a solo career. Cher released 83 singles, with 4 numbers 1, 12 top 10 singles. A legend in the music world.

1967: The Monkees-Davy Jones was the lead singer. The Monkees released three No. 1 singles in 1967, one of which was Daydream. Jones captured the hearts and minds of teenagers all around the world.

1970: The Jackson 5, the first of all groups band to have their first four singles achieves the high spot of the Hot 100. I Want You Back Single was followed by what it was called, Jackson mania.

Marie Osmond is an American singer-actress and family member of the Osmonds. She achieved success as a country pop music artist. Marie produce her first single, Paper Roses," which topped No. 1 on the U.S. chart. From 1976 to 1979, she and her singer brother Donny Osmond hosted the television variety show Donny and Marie.

1971: Donny Osmond seized the world with charm. The 14-year-old launched his first two albums, the Donny Osmond album and To You with Love, Donny, both of which reached 12 and 13, respectively.

1972: David Cassidy was a breakout star from The Partridge Family, a musical sitcom about a family. Cassidy and his on-screen mom (his real-life stepmom) was the only ones singing; the rest of the cast lip-synced. David Cassidy was a sensation; he was everywhere. Girls went crazy with him, buying posters and all kinds of merchandise.

Michael Jackson was an American singer. He went on to a solo career with amazing success. Jackson was dubbed the king of pop. He had many No. 1 hits, like Thriller and Bad, among others. Michael was hunted later in his career by allegations of child molestation.

He died on October 10, 2009, at age 50 of a drug overdose.

1978 John Travolta embodied pure sex appeal as Danny Zuko in the movie Grease and also in Saturday Night Fever, a movie popularizing disco music around the world.

It turned Travolta, then only 24 years old, and his co-star Olivia Newton-John into teenager's idols around the world.

Shawn Cassidy an American singer, actor, writer, and producer. He starred in the television series The Hardy Boys Mysteries, and his albums include Born Late, Under Wraps, Room Service, and Wasp. Cassidy comes from a famous family.

1984: Madonna, the queen of pop at 24 years old, appeared at the 1984 MTV Video Music Awards and rolled over around on stage wearing a wedding dress singing like a virgin. She had many more hits including in 1989 like a prayer.

1990: Mariah Carey is an American singer, song writer, and record producer. Carey soared to fame in 1990 with her album, Mariah Carey. She is famous for the enduring popularity of her holiday music, including 1994's "All I Want for Christmas Is You".

2007: Miley Cyrus, 15 years old, had a Disney Channel show called Hannah Montana. Her debut album as herself, Hannah Montana 2: Meet Miley, debuted at No. 1.

2008: The Jonas brothers were at fever pitch. The brother band enjoyed near-unparalleled success.

Swift Taylor was 18 years old when she released her second album, Fearless, which went on to become the top-selling album of 2009 with hits like "You belong with me.

2010: Justin Bieber fever hit an all-time high when he released his debut album, My World 2.0, in 2010. In 2010, Bieber was probably the epitome of a teen idol.

Section 5

Homeschool planner guide example

Of course, there will be differentiation in elementary, middle, and high school.

Turn lessons into songs.

Kindergarten: Every American learner is familiar with the classic jingle of the ABCs and the reminder of what letter comes after Q. Teachers can use songs and rhymes to help students learn sounds.

Fun with letters: children enjoy copying words out onto papers. Use the child's name and have him or her copy it.

Students learn to read, write, do math, and read the numbers on a clock. Measurement: long and short, wide and narrow, light and heavy. Shapes: circles, triangles, squares, rectangular hexagons, days of the week

Talk about time and weekdays; use vocabulary like five minutes from now, in half an hour is lunch time, this year, last year, and next year. Today is Monday, the first day of the week; yesterday was Sunday; and tomorrow is Tuesday.

Clocks can be made using paper plates and split pins to hold the hands.

Reading is one of the most crucial competencies someone can possess. It allows people to learn new things, explore other cultures, and learn about the world around them.

Use stories to teach reading. Stories are an excellent way to instruct kids to read.

Illustration and big print can help a child recognize the word they are reading.

Tips on how to tutor a child to read:

Focus on letter sounds.

Begin with uppercase letters.

Incorporate phonics

Balance phonics and sight words.

Practice light reading.

Play word games.

These skills are needed by all children in order to learn how to read.

Phonemic awareness: hears and manipulates sounds.

Phonics: recognize between letters and the sounds they make.

Vocabulary: understanding the meaning of the words and definitions

Reading comprehension: understand the meaning of the text or story.

Fluency: ability to read aloud with speed.

Measuring objects: measure objects such as books or tables using body parts like hands or feet. Kids must learn to measure using nonstandard items before they are introduced to standard measurements.

Playing with wooden shapes familiarizes the child with basic geometric shapes.

First grade: Approximately age at 6 or 7-is the age when kids start to comprehend the means of time-the past, present, and future. At the end of first grade, students can count up to 100; do early addition, subtraction, simple reading, write, and do social studies and science.

Clock and times: teach them two ways to show time: analog and digital. One is by reading the hands on a clock, and the other is by reading the numbers on a digital clock.

Explain that digital time can be found on mobile phones, computers, and a car's dashboard.

Second grade: Students learn counting, addition, subtraction up to 100, multiplication, measurements, health, plants, reading comprehension, writing, animals, and about the body.

They also learn about triangles, calculate their faces and edges, and do some geometric calculations.

Third grade: Students learn basic math, subtraction, addition, multiplication, division, science, social studies, history, and language.

Four grade: Students will master addition, subtraction, and multiplication division, fractions with like denominators and less common denominators, and charts, graphs, and tables.

Fifth grade: Includes language arts, math (focusing on adding, subtracting, multiplying, and dividing whole numbers, fractions, and decimals), social studies, science, arts, crafts, and music.

Six grade: Include English, math, place values in whole numbers, Roman numbers, maps with decimal distance, data and graphs, science, and social studies.

Seven grade: Include reading and writing, math, greater common factor, least common factor, and divisibility rules. Square roots, ratios, rates, and proportions; percent; metric measurement

Eighth grade: Math includes problems with whole numbers, decimals, fractions, percentages, square roots, positive and negative square roots, cube roots, dimensional figures, perimeter, area, and classifying polygons, triangles, trapezoids, and quadrilaterals.

Ninth grade: Includes biology, chemistry, science, US history, US government, and world history. Interpret bar graphs, create bar graphs, interpret line graphs, and interpret line plots.

Tenth grade: Include English, language arts, chemistry, algebra, geometry, and world history.

Eleventh grade: Consist of English, math, science, social science, and language. Additionally, algebra, trigonometry, pre-calculus, biology, and chemistry

Twelfth grade: Advanced math, language arts, high-level science, and social studies

Make learning a game; students will become more engaged; connect class material with current events; and students will probably pay more attention when the material is related to what is occurring in the world around them.

Tutors after the catastrophe

Of course, in a SHTF or Teotwawki disaster, teaching kids will take on another perspective. The circumstances are going to be very difficult, and materials to teach will be very scarce.

The person or persons in charge of teaching the youngsters will have to improvise and be very creative to be able to teach using the only resources in their possession. Being a teacher for 30 years, I understand how hard it will be. I know the difficulty tutors or teachers will face with no materials, no blackboard, no papers, or no pencils. They must be very resourceful to improvise and make do with what they have. An incredible, almost impossible situation.

The outline courses above are only a guide for the people in charge of teaching to have an idea of what to teach at each grade level.

People acting as teachers will have a very hard time because of the lack of materials. They are going to have to decide what and how they can teach. Maybe just picking an area or two every day or weekly, wherever they decide or are just able to do it, is sufficient. The most important thing is to prepare the children for the future.

Final thoughts

Hopefully, the information provided here will help you with the mission of keeping your family safe in a catastrophe like Teotwawki-SHTF. Your mission must be a complete effort, mind, body, and spirit.

I hope and pray that a catastrophe like SHTF never happens in our lifetime, but think about it; most of us have Liability car insurance, home insurance, and health insurance, why not prepare for a disaster just in case? The same way we take up others insurances.

Be positive but smart, and just in case create your emergency plan, better to be ready than sorry.

Hopefully you never have to use the techniques and guide in this book, but see it as protection insurance if you ever need it.

In my opinion, humanity is capable of coming together in the event of a disaster to ensure that future generations have better lives.

I like the opportunity again to thanks every survival magazine writers, survival books, as well all those web-sites in the subject, some information presented here is based on conversations I have had with hunters, hikers, Everglades park rangers, military personal, and guerilla underground warriors, whose theories and concepts I have integrated with my own experiences to bring all that information for you the readers.

Keep your eyes and ears open; be ready in case one day the situation gets out of hands, again I hope it never will.

Thank for reading this book!

In order to carry a positive action we must develop here a positive vision.
Dalai Lama

List of SHTF Terminologies

SHTF (shit hit the fan) is a term to describe events that are catastrophic.

WROL-without the rule of law3

BOB- Bug out bag

BOL-bug-out location

BOV-bug-out vehicle

Doomer-a person who believes a worst-case scenario is on its way.

Chow- military expression meaning to sit down and eat. It is interchangeable with mess.

Combat patrol- a group of sufficient size to raid or ambush the enemy

Clearing patrol- a short patrol in order to secure an immediate area.

Standing patrol-a static observation patrol intended to provide early warning

Reconnaissance patrol- usually small, with the mission of gathering information

EDC-everyday carry-wallet, keys, etc.

Teotwawki means the end of the world as we know it.

Thermal imaging-detects radiation emitted by heat instead of light

Infrared technology detects radiation to create a visible image.

IFAK-first aid kit

GHB-Get Home Bag

MRE-meal ready to eat

WWL-world without law

SCOUTING- Observe the terrain and the enemy and find a path through it. Typically, a small group

SAR-search and rescue

NBC-nuclear biologic chemical

CCW-concealed carry weapon

JIC-just in case

EOD -end of days

EOF-escalation of force

EOT-end of times

FIFO-first in, first out

Yoyo, you are on your own.

4WD-four-wheel drive

Homesteading- food security; keeping animals on a piece of land

72-hour kit materials to help you survive 72 hours

Genny-slang for generator

GMO-genetically modified organism

GOOD -Get out of Dodge, is the procedure of getting out of a bad or dangerous situation

HEMP-high altitude electromagnetic pulse-Caused by the detonation of a nuclear weapon.

Ham Radio is a term used to refer to amateur radio.

INCH-is a short message code for family or friends in case you are not coming back home.

Multi-tool, combining other tools.

Military crest-the top of a mountain or hill-a position of tactical advantage

NOAA-the National Oceanic and Atmospheric Administration-provides weather data.

Prepper- is a term to describe an individual who is always prepared.

Patrolling- is a military tactic to achieve a specific objective, like collecting information without being detected and then returning to base.

Castle Doctrine- lessen the duty to retreat

Survival Cache-hidden or secret stash of survival stuff you can access later on.

A survivalist- is a person who has worked on his/her skills to survive outdoor the anticipated breakdown of society.

Low profile- to keep you away from criminals

Blending in- blend into your surrounding

Adaptability- adjust for any situation that may arise

Gauge-measure on the numbers of lead balls-10, 12, 16, 20, and 28

Long term sustainability – ideas to survive in the long run

About the Author

Frank Marchante has been an avid hunter, and has hunted in many different swamps of the everglades thru the state of Florida.

As an educator and a generalist Marchante has read significantly about many topics, and have met extraordinary people, and tried new endeavors. He wanted to experience the world broadly. And he has.

Marchante have been in different parts of the world, and visited many questioned places. He has study history, disasters, emergency planning, and survival strategies to converge into this book. He has received advices from experts and the advices have been filtered through his own experience. The author has had a passion for survival, and evading since he was a very young boy.

Frank has participated in many adventures, accomplishing ascents to one of the tallest peaks, most impressive mountain in Bolivia, 21,000 feet high, Illimani, one of the highest mountain peaks in the Andes, the eighteenth highest peak in South America, using an oxygen mask to reach one of the top summits, walking through the clouds sometimes in the snow all the way pass his knees.

Marchante found thrilling adventure on courage, discipline, and motivation going through rugged remote terrain like in the heart of the Rainforest and dangerous neighborhood to explore and learn to develop his safety system.

The Author ventured deep by foot into the deep, dark, dense, dangerous undergrowth, uninhabitable Amazon Jungle in Bolivia's /Peru one of the wildest dangerous environments on the planet. Drove through the World's Most Dangerous Road Bolivia –The Death Road in 1971.

Frank traveled across the intimidating Titicaca Lake, the highest lake in the world in an Indian canoe, accompanied by an Indian from Bolivia to Peru, 50 years ago, before tourists begins visiting the lake.

He climbed the massive volcano of Popocatepetl, Mexico, the second highest in Mexico and North America's 2nd highest volcano at 5,452 meters (17,887 feet) above sea level. He has also Hang –glide from a very high peak Mountain in Acapulco city and also has done parasailing in Acapulco and Cozumel.

The Author took his first flying lessons in the early 70s in Tamiami airport in South Miami in a Piper Cherokee 140, where at the end of the 80s kept his own plane, a Panther 2 plane. In 1986, he applied to NASA when the Teacher's educator space program to go into space in the shuttle Challenger, he was not chosen. The shuttle exploded 73 seconds after liftoff.

Frank has been an enthusiast of the martial arts since 1964, and has practiced for over 59 years. He began learning karate when he was 13 years old; he later changes style to Wing Chun kun-Fu training, at the same time his father taught him how to box.

The author has always enjoyed racing motorcycles, has owned many through his life and still owns one, a Honda 1970 Bonneville 750cc antique with cruise control.

Frank was one of 30 teachers selected in North America to participate in the People to People Ambassador Program in his delegation and Technical Education advisor to the Republic of China in February 2001. He was a Florida educator, Pear teacher and Head of a Department for 30 years, he is retired now.

He has writing for newspapers and magazines, written several songs, he is the author of published books like Sergio Oliva the Myth, Iron Body -Workout like the Gods-Goddesses of Olympus, Streetwise Extreme-Surviving the Unexpected, El Atentado del Siglo (The Ultimate Target), Marchante Home Inspection, there are many pages on the internet from Russia to France discussing his books.

In 2004, he was the speaker and the recipient of "The Hall of Fame" Award for Sergio Oliva on Feb. 2004, and the speaker who introduced Sergio Oliva at the south Florida Bodybuilding Championship.

His wanderlust led him to explore remote places, like the Amazon Jungle, the Everglades and High Mountain High Peaks.

Photo credit

FreePik.com

Men's walking mountain-silhouette soldier with rifle Kjpargeter-Binoculars. Back cover City skyline in fire-Stockgiu Freepick.com

Pexels.com

Men walking city in dark KoolShooters-men walking on road-Cameron Casey-Men walking with a rifle by Pond Izzet Cakalli-Wearing jacket carrying a rifle Harrison Haines- Photo men walking upstairs-men dark silhouette-flame photo-Escaping thru chain fence. Men warming hands Necip Duman.

Pixabay.com

Men standing on the moon & foot print in the moon wikiImages-dark building space- tunnel Peter Mayer-men walking in cloud silhouette Cocoparisienne-building stair Thefelip- trash containers Dayamay-hall dark door Mertozbagdat-men riding motorcycle dark street Splitshire-dark stair door building 652234- silhouette using bow and arrow Paul S Barlow. Book Cover Men wearing Hoodie-Darksouls1-Book Cover Men Running-MariaD42530 .Back cover Roasting Pixeldust.

Unplash.com

Rabbit Nathan Anderson-Ducks Nikolay Tchaouchev- Wild turkey Suzy Brooks-Pheasant Michael Hoyt-red fox Jeremy Hynes-Wolf close-up howling Philipp Pilz-wolf standing boulder Darren Welsh-Bear coming at you Zdeněk Machácek-eating pig-dove Umang Patel-pigeon-knife cutting branch 2 Bro's Media-hiding jeep pick up Romain Gal-corner trash bags Jon Tyson- plastic bottles on grass Ariungoo Batzoring- big trash bin Kenny Eliason-sidewalk full of trash Yousef Salhamound-train track tunnel Florian Olivo- Lonely dark street by threes Michael Mouritz- lonely alley with trash can Kael Bloom-Motorcycle back tire Himiway Bikes-boat on lake Johny Goerend-Motorcycle in lonely road Volkan Olmez-corner building Heye Jensen-3 men in fog exploring Maël Balland-keep out fence sign Tim Hüfner-wire fence looking out Francisco Galarza.

Unplash.com
Cont.

chicken-first aid kit Kristine Wook-latrine outhouse Robert Linder-latrine outhouse Marcus Ganahi-railroad track Markus Winkler- lonly staircase Stefan Steinbauer-riot Florian Olivo- emty deteriorate garage Jason Mitrione-bicycle night rider Moritz Spahn2-rooster side view Ashes Sitoula-eggs in basket Autumm Mott Rodeheaver-the rooster and the chicken Egor Myznik-dog barking Hassan Pasha-Survival bike horizon Patrick Hendry. Knife cutting branch Markus Spike. Back view men shooting rifle Sebastian Pociecha-trash city corner Jiroe (Matia Rengel) Woman standing in grocery with nuclear mask Nathan Van de Gaaf. Back cover Men in ruin building-Andrew Amistad.

Other photos:

Michelle Marchante photos
Frank Marchante photos
Frank Marchante Jr.

Informational Websites:

www.weather.gov	National Weather Service
www.webmd.com	Medical news and information
www.nhc.noaa.gob	National Hurricane Center
www.nih.gov	National Institutes of Health-information
www.spc.noaa.gov	Storm Prediction Center
www.dhs.gov/national-terrorism-advisory-system -Information	
www.fema.gob	Department of Homeland Security

Gras Publishing Present

Sergio Oliva the Myth

Sergio Oliva, The Myth, the only man to have ever won the Mr. Olympia title uncontested. Now at last Oliva tells all. His early childhood, his daring escape from a communist country to gain his freedom, and how he developed his once in a lifetime, out of this world, Herculean and powerful body with perfect symmetry and mind blowing proportions that made him the most muscular and incredible body of all time. Learn the facts behind the world's most prestigious and famous contests. Get a front row seat as Sergio describes his confrontations with Arnold Schwarzenegger. Nothing is held back as Sergio speaks his mind.

Sergio discusses Bodybuilding Politics, Drugs and more. Find thrilling action and suspense, unlike any other bodybuilder's book, and • Maximum Muscle Development • A Seminar with Sergio-Over 100 Q & A's • Sergio Oliva's Training Secret Routines • Steroids-GH, Interaction of Growth Hormone • Get in Shape Routines for Women • The Myth's Health Recipes.

Gras Publishing Present

Iron Body
Workout like the Gods, Goddesses of Olympus

You'll discover how to:

Men: Go from fat or skinny to being muscular. Build a bullet proof fighter body, stay lean and hard, combine cardio and weight training, accelerate muscle grow, GH and steroids, nutrition advice. Gain massive 25 pounds of muscle. No special equipment required. The hard gainer solution.

Women: Become lean; obtain a bikini, tight, sexy body with a toned ass and lean legs. Shape your body at any age. Goodbye to diets and calories. Secrets for beauty. Vanish cellulite!

No special equipment is needed.

Included are isometric exercises, jogging, sprinting, Power Twister, Strands/Spring Expander, band exercises, Aerobics-Calisthenics-Fat-Burning Furnace, gym rules, how to choose one, Heavy Duty, Mass Training, Force Reps, Pyramid System, Intensity, Down the Rack, Hammer and Sled Workout, Medicine Ball, Flip Tires, Overhead Weight, Bucket Walks, Crawling, etc

Gras Publishing Present

Streetwise Extreme
Surviving the unexpected

This book will teach you:

How to prevent and deal with the most common attacks against women and man, in an elevator, parking lot, your car, driving, at the mall, at the bank, at the ATM, home invasion, traveling abroad, in a public restroom, riding a bus, plus ….

Using verbal techniques to stop a confrontation
How to place an emergency call
Woman college safety -Sorority- Fraternity -Sexting
How to defend against attempted rape
Date rape drugs
Cyber safety–Identity Theft- Medical identity theft
Meet someone on the web without any danger
How the Street Predator thinks and Act
Dangerous Cities/ USA Neighborhood, sucker punch
Terrorism- Mass shooting- Hostage-Lone Wolf
Flash-Mob Riot-Hijacking
Legal issues in Self -Defense
Stand your ground-Retreat-Castle Doctrine
Recognize a dangerous person or situation
Learn how to defend yourself to win a Violent Encounter
Plus much more ……….

Gras Publishing Present

El Atentado del Siglo

BY FRANK MARCHANTE

Un trama trepidante y llena de suspenso..... Caracterización intrigante.
Basado en una historia real, alterado con algo de ficticia, toma a los lectores de sorpresa, llena el corazón de suspenso y angustioso pulso, fuerte, ya sea en tierra o en el mar. Este suspenso de gran éxito, se establece a 90 millas de USA.

Un hombre de la CIA infiltrado en Cuba con una misión para ajusticiar a Fidel Castro, un hombre con un dedo en el gatillo de su arma puede cambiar la historia.....
Repleto de acción, suspenso y los personajes reales, humanos con una caracterización increíble.

El autor de este apasionante relato, cuya identidad, por razones obvias, debe permanecer en secreto contó su historia a Frank Marchante que lo trajo a la vida, trasfirió, le añadió alguna ficticia y organizo en papel. Los nombres a través del libro son igualmente ficticios por la misma razón.
No importa si todos los datos son ciertos o no. Emocionante e imaginativa, llena de acción y la intriga aumenta el pulso, teniendo a lectores en una aventura salvaje.

No es ningún secreto que la CIA estuvo involucrada en una variedad de proyectos, para llevar a cabo la eliminación de Fidel Castro. Este es un relato fascinante en primera persona de un proyecto de la CIA para eliminar a Fidel Castro, de la realización de una acción encubierta en secreto que detalla las mentiras y engaños de la agencia.

Una de la mayor acción jamás encubierta y en secreto realizada. Se lee casi como una novela de suspenso y aventura. Incluye crónica de la Revolución de los últimos 55 años, también presenta parte de la historia de cuba.

Notes

www.ingramcontent.com/pod-product-compliance
Lightning Source LLC
Chambersburg PA
CBHW032035150426
43194CB00006B/280